COACHING THE

FLEXIBLE MAN-TO-MAN DEFENSE

Coaching the

Flexible

Man-to-Man Defense

AUBREY R. BONHAM

Parker Publishing Company, Inc. West Nyack, N.Y.

Library of Congress Cataloging in Publication Data

Bonham, Aubrey R
  Coaching the flexible man-to-man defense.

  Includes index.
    1. Basketball--Defense. 2. Basketball coaching.
I. Title.
GV888.B66   796.32'32   78-18417
ISBN 0-13-139170-4

DEDICATION

To all the young men whose work and play on the basketball court strengthened my teaching knowledge of the game, and to the loyal fans, and to the coaches against whom we competed. To my wife whose help was immeasurable and to our family whose loyalty has never failed.

What This Defense Will Do for You

Coaching the Flexible Man-to-Man Defense highlights the very important details of skill learning that take your players beyond average defense to a solid, well-disciplined, complete, and aggressive pressure defense that wins games.

Flexible man-to-man defense adds to the mobility of each player. Constant position changes will counter offensive moves of both the man and the ball. With flexible defense your team will use new movements and positions without tying itself to the old method of staying between the man and the basket. Flexible motion can be used at all times to adjust constantly the position of your defender between the man and the ball in the keyhole areas.

During my years of high school coaching, where the fundamentals of flexible man-to-man defense were developed and executed, the win record was as impressive as the success I had with it on the college level. This makes me certain that this flexible man-to-man defense works at the high school level today.

In fact this book came out of questions from high school coaches who keep asking me among other questions: "What are the necessary steps to take to successfully emphasize the flexible man-to-man defense in my program?"

Flexible man-to-man defense instruction starts from scratch with stance, movement, spacing, and the positioning of the defensive man according to the offensive floor problems. It also gives high priority to constant body shuffle motion while defending until your team gets possession of the ball. This positioned body has continuous motion any place on the court even when the opponent is standing still.

Step by step this flexible defense movement will counter the problems of position on the perimeter, the baseline, the side court, the front court, and the post. This concept places the flexible indi-

7

vidual defender in a team relationship of two on two; three on three; four on four; and five on five.

This requires a multiple set of operating team moves. These are synchronized with team motion tactics to counter the attempts of the offense to penetrate the defense perimeter.

The efficient flexible tools of each player pressure the offense together with added pressures from the combined and correlated team skills.

You can follow the coaching steps from stance through individual detailed skill learning of positions. And on to the steps of teaming two or more defenders to tie their positions and motions together, thus giving each defender greater mobility and help by adding new team skills which are basic to improving your complete team defense.

Special floor defensive patterns are presented after the team defense has countered the set and breaking offense patterns.

The drills in the book take direct aim at emphasizing superior skills with the goal of *over-learning* to achieve perfection in the execution of the tools of position, movement, and spacing.

Such defensive problems as controlling running lanes, forcing cutter moves away from screens, countering the play timing, and rolling off screens, are explained and diagrammed.

Also emphasized is flexible positioning which calls for constant movement by the defender. He adjusts his spacing to counter screens and to help teammates without losing a good guarding position on his basic assignment. This positioning helps your team get positions that will handle the offensive tactics and react quickly to stop other counter moves. It takes quick collapsing moves and faster recovery moves to maintain command of the offensive action.

Tempo will be considered. Never forget the opposition's tempo in ball and player movement. You may be countering the offensive team tempo well, but if your defensive tempo does not increase to correspond to the offensive tempo, you allow the offense to get non-pressure shots.

Another area included in this book is shot pressure. Better high school shooting from the eighteen to twenty-two foot areas makes it essential for the defense to put shot pressure on scoring attempts and to do so without losing the baseline defense while pressuring to keep opponents from penetrating.

Effort is made to stick to the drilling of details that give a step-by-step defense learning opportunity to increase the toughness of your defensive instruction.

It is certain that this flexible man-to-man defense will develop in your players an attitude of concentration and of learning from within the individual disciplines necessary to gain advanced skill in all departments of the game. The flexible man-to-man defense is a solid base upon which you can establish game winning results.

Aubrey R. Bonham

Contents

Legend for Court Moves and Court Divisions

⟶	Player movement path
◂- - -	Ball movement path
◂〜〜	Dribble movement path
〜〜◓↓	Dribble reverse and hand-off move
〜〜▸	Dribble fake reverse
◯—┼—▸ X—┼—▸	Defenders' point position relationships
◯〜〜〜▸	Fake & Dribble
—〱—	Defenders' pressure fake
⟶┤	Screen move
////////	Defender's hand pressure
◓	Offense man with ball

Nomenclature for Drills

◯	offense;
X	defense;
⊥	player position relationships
∿	fake reverse
⊞	stops
∿➤	full reverse
+	front cross
//	change of pace
▽	release
•	ball
C⊃	reverse pivot
⊥	player position)

1

Flexible Man-to-Man Defense
Preparation

Flexible defense should not be confused with the mechanical rule of position, spacing, and movement. Real flexible defense does not have an inhibition for player and team defense. Flexible defense encompasses all position variations to put the most pressure on the offense's basic moves in their scoring patterns and shot positions.

Flexible defense players should use constant spacing changes for positions of offensive player assignment. Flexible defense spacing reacts to the position of the ball at all times, to changing positions of the offensive player in relation to the basket and the floor.

Flexible defense is elastic and experimental. It quickly ferrets out the strong player and the team moves, then adjusts quickly to put the greatest pressure against the number one moves of individual and team offense.

Flexible defense shuts off the inside moves and places more than one pressure on offensive moves.

A ball out of your vision makes it impossible for you to react in a positive move. This forces you to counter after opposition moves.

The experiences of most coaches in coaching defensive basketball brings them, as it did me, to an early conclusion that success must be based on the perfection of the fundamental skills. If the basic part of your game is to be defense then defense preparation is vitally important.

Flexible man-to-man defense became important to me during the early years of coaching basketball. After attending a summer basketball clinic I brought back the fast break philosophy to the college. Its use caused an immediate increase in the offense's success but it also increased the opposition's scoring. We did not appreciate running just to stay even with our opposition.

I decided to work for a quick team drop away from the basket after the shot and to pressure the ball advance over the full court. This was not the orthodox defense of just positioning against the man and doing little more than delaying the advance of the ball.

We wanted to play the ball at all times and to keep constant pressure on all close pass lanes to the ball. Our main objective was to keep between our offense assignment and the ball but not to lose contact. The defense had to help at all times against the ball, read the offense position, and anticipate the pass potential. All players had to concentrate on keeping the ball out of the court center and on dropping back to the key defense, as well as using every opportunity to drive the ball down the sidelines.

Our success was immediate, and the fast break began to give us a run of points without our opponents developing an immediate point answer. From this point on we worked on flexible defense moves to counter all patterns by sliding away from the shooting area and going over the top man-to-man with help on the ball side without any switches. Our players were sold on defense which made our success into a tradition of winning for twenty-nine years.

COACH'S APPROACH TO DEFENSE LEARNING

You, as a coach, will soon see that the flexible skills of the defensive game can be called the *tools of defense* to be developed to control or counter the offensive moves of the opponent. The development of these tools cover defensive player positions in many different floor situations.

Your individual defense moves should develop flexibility in your players in order to counter ball position changes, player floor changes, and other team combination moves.

You create individual responsibility by giving the defensive player greater flexibility to perfect the moves. The additional defensive tools give the player greater mobility which demands hard work, patience, and intense concentration.

Tool learning in flexible defense challenges the capabilities of each player and calls for capacity conditioning in order to keep skill tones at a maximum level throughout the entire game.

The flexing positions on the ball and ballside away from the ball *with spacing* are the ultimate tools to counter the individual or team patterns. Maximum concentration on the defense skills must be brought to bear to counter the screen picks.

As the coach you are responsible for a good selling job on the necessary discipline needed by the defenders to counter offensive reactions while playing defense by the inch.

Flexible man-to-man defense action has multiple positions with many individual decisions to be made in split second positioning.

This defense gives the individual player great freedom in playing the ball and the man over the court. It means the learning of many moves to counter the offensive action. The responsibility of counter decisions must be developed in each defensive player.

Coaching this defense takes great patience because of its flexibility in movement, spacing, and positioning.

The requirements for establishing the flexible defense must challenge the defenders' physical and mental capacities to develop the flexible tools that will offset the differences in players' skills.

It is better not to weight the requirements. A weakness in any phase of the basics of flexible man-to-man defense could produce the flaw that would lead to failure.

FLEXIBLE MAN-TO-MAN REQUIREMENTS

Discipline. Flexible man-to-man defense requires more discipline in learning and in development to successfully counter basic patterns of the offense.

Ball Position. Such movements must consider the ball position at all times along with man position in floor relationships. To think and see ahead of offensive moves, a player must have knowledge of team moves through rapid court changes.

The normal procedures and drills for defense development may not provide all the counter answers to control the offenses. Flexible man-to-man defense goes far beyond the positioning of a man according to the basket and the floor situation.

This defense must take ball position on every opponent and contest every move and every pass lane the opposition attempts.

Emphasis on Details. Greater attention must be placed on the details found within the skills to create the greatest possible success in countering the offense.

Drills. Your basic skill drills must emphasize the fact that this approach is the quickest, best, and most efficient road toward perfecting the flexible moves. Your helpside drill should be set up to show absolute help and absolute roll-back to cover your players' basic assignment pass lane. The following drill illustrates the importance of detail in skill instruction. It points up the need for sound defensive tools that lead step by step to the ultimate goal of total defense.

Diagram 1-1. This illustrates helpside: two-on-two high key position. X1 has responsibility against the ball and should take away the right hand drive to the basket which is the dribbler's best move. X1 should be ready to close the inside dribble to the key quickly with a position to pressure the shot or to pressure the inside pass lane. X2 should be a step inside toward the ball and back ready to put a quick stop move on O1 while at the same time be ready to drop back on his assignment covering possible pass lane all the way. X1 and X2 can assume outside positions to force the ball inside if their strong moves are outside. The further away from the basket the guard roll sits the more drop X2 should make.

Diagram 1-2. This is a medium post two-on-two weak-side cut. Close into the basket on the weak side. X2 guard can play the pass lane, two-time, and roll in shutting off the inside lane.

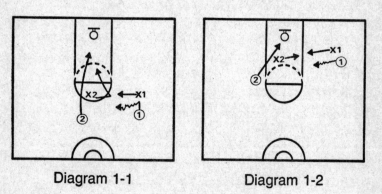

Diagram 1-1   Diagram 1-2

Diagram 1-3. Perimeter two-on-two. Outside guard positions to force the ball toward the sideline and the baseline, also keeps the ball on the weakest side of the offensive pattern. X2 should play pass lane with a deeper drop to cover O2 if he breaks.

A great deal of time should be used in the *preparation* of the

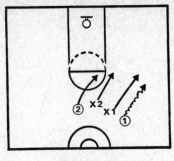

Diagram 1-3

drills and time-saving organization. Review your defense drills frequently. Try to improve and *check results* as the season progresses.

Be flexible. Do not allow yourself to get mechanically oriented. Don't think that all players will come through the drills completely equipped to handle the offensive problems.

QUESTIONS FOR DEFENSE INSTRUCTION

There are common individual and squad errors that need the coach's careful attention. Coaching these areas successfully calls for the best selling approach that coaching and teaching can devise.

The learning axiom, "Don't make the same mistake twice," must have emphasis, and the rote opportunity of specific flexible skill practice to counter each mistake. Flexible skill should be overlearned by rote in order to withstand the game pressure reactions.

To review your defensive drills and instructions the simplest way to bring your thoughts and experiences together is to question each procedure. The following questions will help you to review your own skill patterns and to point up the details for successful teaching of flexible man-to-man defense.

1. Does your defense instruction build the defender's skill ·tools to give him a variety of moves to counter the offense?
2. Does your instruction teach decision responsibility in choosing the counter moves by the defender?
3. Are the defenders aware of the number of practice opportunities to increase skill in a five-minute drill?

4. Do your practice drills follow an orderly approach from basic skills to total defensive moves, to slow down or to control the offense pattern?

5. Will your drill repetitions in the defensive tool developing process allow for mental as well as physical maturity?

6. Can you walk away from a drill when results are not positive and at the next practice hit it hard again? Failure builds up negative tensions. Come back hard after a rest. See if you aren't more successful.

7. Do you have a positive atmosphere for your drills? Player confidence is a big plus. Relaxed players are able to go all out to interpret and execute details.

8. Does your player preparation for the drill always instill the desired readiness for an all-out try?

9. Does your hustle atmosphere keep greediness and laziness at a minimum?

10. Do you have the answer to mental and mechanical errors? One big answer is: *drill, drill, drill,* until the players have overlearned the execution of details that spell success.

11. Will your drill take care of slow learners by having enough flexibility to add or subtract from the drill and yet not lose the drill's primary objective?

12. Do you rate each player's background experiences to find his ability to concentrate over a period of time?

13. Do you have variety in your drills to slow down or pick up the tempo of your practice?

14. Do your players realize that executing a skill once in practice does not mean it is over-learned and ready for game pressure?

15. If your player cannot react to floor pressure do you continue the practice drill until results begin to show automatically in his game?

16. When your player realizes an error will your practice give him maximum opportunity to concentrate on a vigorous, determined try to eliminate the error *now*?

17. Does your squad enjoy penalties to tone and improve the various skills of the practice program? Example: Shooting-contest losers running for endurance, lateral shuffles, rebounds, etc.

18. Do you emphasize squad peer recognition in the execution of good skills for individual players?
19. Do your players analyze their skill failures and try for better execution the next time?
20. Does your drill actually increase the confidence of each player so that he goes all out on each try?
21. Do you maintain a game tempo throughout your drill practice? Keep away from learning levels?
22. Do you challenge your players to leave the floor each day with the certainty their playing ability has improved?
23. Does your practice minimize the fear of failure and emphasize all-out effort to out-practice your opponents in preparation for a game win?

PLAYERS' CONTRIBUTIONS TO FLEXIBLE DEFENSE

Player input into the development of flexible defense must be sold to each individual defender. He is responsible for his contributions toward developing the flexible defense.

Accepting the Challenge. There is a real challenge to the physical capabilities and the mental concentration of players learning the flexible defense fundamentals which creates an intense desire to be the very best defensive team. As such, the squad should have confidence, for it has accepted the challenge to pay a higher price in practice sessions than the opposition.

The day your defenders execute quick defense changes to floor pressures your coaching has become successful.

Eager to Improve. When you select your defenses according to a squad's present ability and experience, *make sure that the weekly practice schedule puts the emphasis on the maximum development of each player.* This is the master goal of flexible defense.

Willing to Make Maximum Effort. An all-out hustle habit in playing flexible defense covers many errors made by inexperienced players.

I found over the years of successful high school and college coaching that well-learned and executed flexible defense was the primary factor in a squad's consistent winning.

Forcing Opponents. Remind your players that there are great compensations from forcing opponents to play beyond a normal pace throughout the game. The opponents' efficiency fades with even a partial loss of playing condition. The opponents' concentration and confidence begin to lessen, making defense problems easier to counter.

Being Confident. An all-out effort on defense is very satisfying to the ego. It builds the confidence that creates greater relaxation so necessary to continue the all-out flexible defensive play.

Players know when they have been properly prepared to counter the opposition's offensive moves. The harder you work on the flexing moves, the more consistent your defensive game becomes. This eliminates the fear of failure. Some players talk themselves into a fear of failure rather than any fear forming from the opposition's pressure.

Any team may find itself squandering the home floor advantage by relaxing from too much confidence, or by wanting to make a superior personal showing before the home crowd. Sometimes your team begins to play better away from home. This is a sign of a good team, but the team should develop the same attitude and concentration for home floor games. Ask yourself whether your home game preparation has the same approach as your away from home preparation.

The tightening up of a player under pressure may come from concentrating too much on his own game. Team thinking could be the answer. Tell him to ask himself: "What are my teammates contributing to the game?" Team thinking may help to shake the tenseness from his game.

OBSERVATIONS OF HIGH SCHOOL WEAKNESSES

The charting of the most frequent and common individual and team errors found in several high schools in three leagues pointed up the *weaknesses of spacing and positioning on both the ball and the man*. There was little consistency—over and over the same glaring, specific weaknesses occurred.

Fouling. Do you put special emphasis on cutting down the number of times your opposition goes to the free throw line?

Errors Caused by Inexperience. Inexperienced players who have a short concentration period must be carried by your coaching skill until they have had some success with the new moves.

The mastery of the flexible man-to-man defense depends upon

superior stance, position, spacing, and movement *under game pressure*. The human equation of the squad is an important key, as is your ability to lead and guide the mental and physical forces of the team.

When a player realizes an error, will the drill session give him many opportunities to concentrate on vigorous, determined tries to eliminate the error *now?*

Players should be made aware of daily development in their defense skill. Point up a specific weakness for each practice and work for improvement.

Lack of Intensity and Concentration. Players each week should recognize improvement in their practice intensity and concentration. Such development should last longer with each week's practice. Keep in mind that defense will last some forty seconds on each turnover. Players should look at defense as the time it takes to force the offense to turn the ball over, not on thirty-two minute game pacing approaches.

Lack of Emotional Control. Remind your players that there is a thin line between getting up for their best effort and in tightening up defensive reactions by allowing a mental overemphasis.

Constant practice in highly competitive situations helps the player to eliminate emotional control weaknesses. Good emotional control insures the most efficient use of the defensive skill tools.

Players should be taught the officials' role in the game. Teach your players never to use any action that draws the officials' personal attention. Always let the officials divide their attention among the nine other players as well.

Teach them that good players always have a competitive fire in their boilers that is personally controlled by a fool-proof valve.

OFFENSE VS. DEFENSE PSYCHOLOGY

I would rather have the opponent's defenses bothering my offense than have the opponent's offense crippling my defensive players' confidence in their own defensive plan.

Coaches seldom have problems preparing their offense for the opposition. Their major game preparation weakness is failure to spend the time in practice to physically and mentally groove the defense moves to counter the opposition's pattern.

How many times has your squad played hard defense over a 20

to 40 second period only to make a silly mistake in the next second
to throw away a fine defensive effort which can never be recovered
in the game?

Resting on Defense. Players fall into the trap of resting on defense. This habit destroys more good defensive play than any other
error. Players should develop the spirit of forcing the offense to
give up the ball in a few seconds, get possession of it themselves
and *then* rest if necessary.

Lack of Pressure and Fast Tempo in First Quarter. If your
players don't put steady pressure on the offense and set the tempo
high throughout the first quarters of the game they may be in
trouble. Coach them to force the offense to over-pace in the early
stages of the game which will cause its tempo to slow down in the
later stages. This will hamper or eliminate your opponents' attack
efficiency.

Fear of Forcing Opponents to Dribble. Never allow your
players to be afraid to force their opponents to dribble. A good
team defense should never be broken by a dribble or one-on-one
play. Forcing the offense to dribble destroys the pass pattern attack
and thus takes quick team movement away from the offense.

The team must realize that half of its losses could be attributed to
the free throw scoring of the opposition.

In observing a number of high school practices, I noticed that
handwork, spacing, and position drills were almost completely ab-
sent from the defense sessions.

Little pressure seemed to be put on players to keep away from
the third foul in the first two quarters. In games where the player
was playing with the third foul, his defense seemed to drop off
heavily when pressuring the opponent.

Stripping the Ball. Some defensive players put too much emphasis on stripping the ball from the opposition. This gives the
crowd an extra thrill. But the defensive move is successful about
one in six tries. The five misses put the opposition at the free throw
line or in the sixty-percent shot area. This also puts the defender in
early foul trouble.

Controlled hand action and a good position to force the offensive
player to open the ball to clean hand action produces the best
results in the long run.

Not Knowing Official Rules. Do your players know the rules?

Do they execute their defensive skills according to official interpretation?

Many players are confused by the officials' calls. And some coaches' sideline reactions can mean a difference in interpretation. More pre-season get-togethers of officials and coaches would be worthwhile. This would help to understand official interpretation. Be aware of the gray areas in interpretation and prepare your defenders, thus insuring the greatest confidence in their flexible defense play.

Lack of Training for Overloading. The defensive player who assumes an overload on defense must be efficient in releasing and recovering before the offense can take advantage of the movement.

Overloading the defender gives flexibility to the players' defensive actions in contesting extra pass lanes or in halting the ball's offensive penetration.

Carelessness. My observations of several tournaments showed me a marked carelessness by the defense in executing proper spacing, position, and ball contesting. The defensive pressure seemed to be a go-for-broke-close-in with intimidation as the chief objective.

Zone teams forced out of the basic defense showed a complete lack of expanded team effort to pressure the ball with man-to-man defense. The usual outcome seemed to be breakaway baskets by the opposition and a general march to the free throw line.

Do your rebound drills give you a continuous improvement in the check-out timing and the ball recovery drive?

Lack of Condition. Keep your stats on the effectiveness of your flexing defense pressure through four quarters. Be sure your conditioning program for defensive play keeps pressure on in the fourth quarter. Tempo stays up and the spacing stays in when the team is in top defense condition. Flexible defense places greater emphasis on superior condition to sustain the necessary concentration, emotional stress, and physical work output.

Not Enough Drills. Do you place your heavy work drills strategically throughout your daily practice? Watch the pace of your practice and have some quick pick-up action drills ready to insert.

Your drilling must go beyond just gaining the skill. It needs continuous review if you want the tone to remain high week after week.

Be sure to check your drills carefully if your practice hits a slow learning period. Consider whether the skill is too advanced. Is the drill using too many skills while trying to emphasize one skill area?

Not Enough Emphasis on Perfecting Skills. Skill teaching stations with one skill practice at each basket for a ten minute period can give players extra opportunity to work on their weaknesses. Players can move from station to station. The station skills can be changed from time to time depending on the scrimmage or game weaknesses they may show.

A player in skill learning competition may hit a resistance plateau if he is falling behind his teammates. This may be eliminated by an extra few minutes of personal attention.

During the learning of skill in building the habit to react to game pressure, players may revert to old and less efficient skill habits. This requires more drill and experience to make the new skill stronger than the old.

2

Developing Flexible Skills
to Counter Individual Offensive Moves

The offensive player is developing highly specialized moves that he is executing with speed and efficiency. Therefore the flexible defensive player must have specialized and efficient tools to counter these moves.

The defensive tool development cannot be left to chance but must develop the positions that will counter specific offensive moves. Flexible tools should balance the footwork, the hand pressure, the anticipation, the position and the spacing, and have an intensity equal or surpassing the offensive threat.

The counter skill is the result of research on ball position, man position, floor position, and possible pass lanes to teammates. We assume that this skill will counter the good offensive move *but* may have to be altered when confronted by highly specialized nonconforming offensive skills. Solid percentage success is found in the use of this counter skill tool.

Individual offensive details such as ball position change by the dribbler, faking ability, change of speed, the screen, and the two-way break of play are considered in each counter skill move. Each offensive player executing the similar move may cause defenders to make a slight adjustment to offset their opponents' personal execution of the skill. This variable approach to counter offensive moves carries the title of flexible man-to-man defensive play.

FLEXIBLE MAN-TO-MAN DEFENSE CONCEPTS

Your defensive man's proper position is one that controls the running lanes to the basket the cutter might use, and one that pressures the pass lanes of the opponent moving toward the basket

29

or ball. This skill cuts down the offensive man's ability to penetrate the defense with or without the ball.

There will be continuous reference to the flexible defense pressure being placed on the ball first and then on the man covering various floor positions. *The ball position at all times will key your spacing and position work against the man.*

Remember basketball defense is played by *inches* over a time period averaging about *thirty to forty seconds* before the ball is turned over. Earlier man-to-man defense was locked into the straight one-on-one.

DEVELOPING TEAM DEFENSES

Earlier zone defenses flourished with several variations for positioning the defensive team to stop penetration. But man-to-man never lost its soundness for defending one man against an opponent of similar physique and reaction qualities, and in assuming individual defense responsibilities in relationship to his teammates.

All zones had specific weaknesses, especially an inability to expand for large court coverage. Further weaknesses show when defense is forced to leave a primary strength to go to a secondary defense. Teams with sound fundamental man-to-man techniques always played the toughest zone because they defended in their zone both the *man* and the *pass* with greater tool knowledge and execution.

The combination of the *man-to-man* concept with the *zone* concept came into being as switching and matching defenses. With the offense developing more variations, the defense had to come up with greater flexibility from the basic move in order to cope with these new offensive problems.

The strict basic man-to-man position play has retreated in favor of defense positions which place the greatest pressure on each offensive situation.

The flexible concept involves a combination of positions, spacing, and moves taken from all the defensive team forms such as zones, switches, and man-to-man.

The specific talents of the offense compared to the collective and individual defensive strengths that can be brought to bear on that offense will be the deciding factor in choosing the defensive game plan.

This decision is based upon the capabilities of the defensive team and on one that will enhance the success of each individual player in carrying out his assignment.

You, as a coach, may choose the right plan of defense to control the offense but you may lack players with individual ability and experience to make the plan successful.

Sometimes players are blamed for the lack of success but a little more research on defensive plans would show that other plans might fit the players' experience and abilities better and give the team an opportunity to control a particular pattern successfully.

Unforeseeable factors of human emotional concentration and intensity on any given night can smash the best plans. It is better to have a plan that places all the team's combined abilities in the most strategic positions. Any one game plan or a portion may have to be adjusted or dropped in the first minutes of the game. Always have a secondary defensive plan to switch to in case of a primary defensive breakdown caused by a personnel change or a new offensive move. This consideration is most important and has paid off in the experiences of many coaches.

Just making a shift of assignments or changes in spacing and positioning may upset the offenses' only plan of attack, thus taking away its momentum and giving the defense successful control.

MECHANICS OF FLEXIBLE MOVES TO BE PERFECTED

The mechanics of the starting stance has been a coaching controversy for some time. This has led to some confusion in establishing the best possible body position for *each* defensive player.

General mechanics with minor variations could be successfully developed by players with natural speed and quickness. This superior native ability combined with hustle can cover a multitude of sins. Just think how much further this same player with disciplined mechanics could develop as a defensive standout when he has perfection as his ultimate goal.

Mechanics of Motion

Mechanics should consider foot spread, weight balance, arm and hand positions, flex position, spacing, and body tensions. This is basic to pressure defense against ball and potential receivers.

Coaches used to drill all players with the same stance regardless of player strength, reaction time, height, body maturity, or physical type. But today the stance and position should have degrees of flexibility that enhance the individual needs of *each* player and make the defender better able to cope with all the new offensive innovations. Keep in mind the constant improvement of players against the most efficient offense skills.

Start your stance drill practice with one general body position. Flex the stance according to the needs of each individual player at this learning stage. Keep a flexible point of view to allow changes as the player gains experience and becomes stronger. Have defenders near key and basket recognize the extra danger by double timing their reactions in defensing in the area. Be sure to have players exchange floor positions after several moves.

Full squad assume positions in three rows far enough apart to have good shuffle room.

Diagram 2-1. This illustrates Follow the Leader with a quick player executing lateral and vertical shuffles.

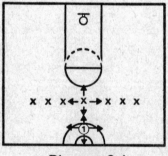

Diagram 2-1

Diagram 2-2. This places two passers in front of squad moving the ball slowly, then speeding up, using a quick single dribble.

Diagram 2-2

FOOT POSITIONS FOR SHUFFLE MOVES

Foot positions that give the best balance, quickest reaction, and quickest stops, should be turned slightly toward the direction you want to travel. Turning the feet too far in this direction will make you a count slower in reversing that direction.

Naturally if opponent speeds beyond your shuffle capabilities, your shuffle must turn into a run to gain or keep position.

A defender who makes few mistakes has developed controlled foot positions successfully countering offensive moves.

The lateral shuffle is the easiest shuffle movement to learn and should be a starting place when teaching defensive motion. The stop, start, stop, change of lateral direction has almost a simultaneous foot-stop and push-off in the opposite direction. The lead leg coming into the stop is cocked ready for the push with the instant thrusting against the floor forcing a quick change of direction. Be sure the lead foot in the motion direction is working slightly ahead of the lead shoulder.

The shuffle change of direction is executed with both feet pushing in unison to accelerate the body for a change of direction. Stutter-stepping has one foot thrust at a time which puts inferior limits on movement and on body control.

There should be *no* bobbing up and down of the shoulders in the shuffle motions. Body flex keeps the shoulder height even or slightly under the offensive man's shoulders. Work off the inside of the feet with weight balanced on the balls of the feet.

The shuffle is kept as close to the floor as possible in the move-

ment. There can be no stop or change of direction with the feet off
the floor. If you are advancing with the left foot forward and the
right foot back, you should get a maximum push-off from the inside
of the foot over the great toe. Reverse action with right foot forward.

ADVANCE AND RETREAT STEP SKILLS

The advance and retreat step is the most difficult to master.
While teaching this movement you should be patient, yet be em-
phatic.

The center of gravity position should swing between the front
and back foot. Think of this balancing shift of weight between the
feet while shuffling as similar to a pendulum swing—never quite
getting to either front or back foot.

The player shifting gravity balance while executing the shuffle
advance with quick shuffles must not get his balance caught too far
forward as he advances. Such a forward weight position could cost
two counts before he starts a new directional change. Some coaches
think it is more aggressive to allow the weight shift to come over
the advanced foot. Some coaches have players shift their weight to
the back foot for quicker release to cover the cutter. To advance,
use a back foot thrust as the lead leg is lifted and shifted forward.
Reverse this procedure as you retreat. A major thrust back is made
by the front foot with almost an instant thrust-lift-pull-back by the
rear foot.

This foot position and body balance maintained inside the feet
gives you the best control while keeping the ankle strain at a
minimum.

Diagram 2-3. This shows foot positions on defensive moves to
control the ball movement by the dribbler in several floor positions.

Hand pointing to the inside hip is always important. The No. 1
position forces the dribble to the right with a lateral shuffle, keeping the inside hand pointed at the dribbler's inside hip. He should
not overshift to the ball and get burned with a reverse. No. 2 angles
his position to force the dribbler down the side to eliminate the
inside reverse, and pressure him to stop the baseline drive to the

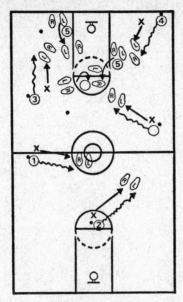

Diagram 2-3

basket. The No. 3 position is a left side dribble down to the corner. Never let the dribbler get a baseline drive position. Space away from the dribbler to eliminate a reverse drive. No. 4 has a tough assignment to eliminate good corner shooters and force the dribbler up. Never allow a baseline drive. Start the opponent up on the angle. Maintain the pressure up but don't overplay to allow a reverse drive.

No. 5 shows the inside post defensive position against player O5 with the ball in three positions. Low post O5 has the ball on the right side at the baseline. Defender steps with his left foot in front and his left arm extended. This allows an opportunity to get back to the board. Fronting will cut him off from the board. The right side medium post has the ball high on O5's left side. His left foot and arm should be in front. His right foot is back to protect a loop pass under. He should shift to a forcing-out position if the ball gets into receiver O5. X5 positions right side of the high post. X5 takes an inside position with his right foot high, his left foot back. This gives him a chance to tag a poor pass-in. He should shift his feet to stop a baseline drive if the ball is getting in.

LATERAL MOTION

The diagrams will consider the body, foot, and arm positions to counter the offense's best lateral moves.

Spacing is Mr. King—the real counter on drives.

Hard ballside position is maintained by foot position and movement.

Diagrams 2-4 to 2-9 show the lateral defensive shuffle action used to counter the dribbler's lateral action of stops, starts, fake drives, fake pull-backs, fake reverses, and the front cross. The hand is always pointing at the inside hip.

Diagram 2-4. This is a change of pace. Defender's position is one with shoulders ahead. A fake reverse by opponent tries to get the defender to shift his position. The defender releases eight inches more spacing, then applies pressure.

Diagram 2-5. Dribbler starts and stops to throw the defender out of position.

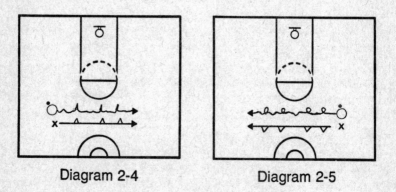

Diagram 2-4   Diagram 2-5

Diagram 2-6. The defender faking a reverse must release deep enough to gain a new pressure position.

Diagram 2-7. This is a change of speed to get the defender off balance and a reverse. Concentration and intensity help the defender to maintain position. The dribbler works on an angle and then pulls back.

Diagram 2-8. The defender's inside hand should always be in a position to slap the front cross again. When executed, the defender must release and get a new position. Overplaying the direction of the dribbler always opens the front cross move. The defender has to release to gain back a pressure position—the key for defense.

Diagram 2-9. Similar to 2-8 with a deeper angle.

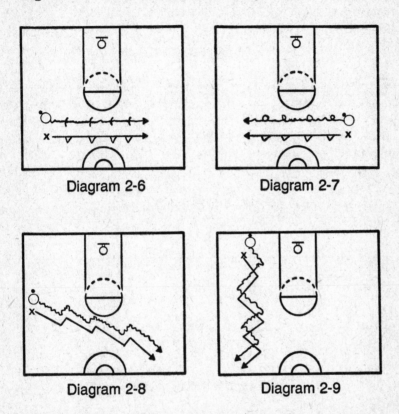

Diagram 2-6   Diagram 2-7

Diagram 2-8   Diagram 2-9

Defensive tools will be referred to in several floor situations together with offensive pattern problems. By using the more flexible defensive tools you add to the defender's confidence and create a stronger psychological approach to this phase of the total game.

Successful position play throughout the time the ball is in the possession of the offense is based on several tools that help the constant interchange in positioning.

A defensive tool should be considered as any movement that takes care of a specific offensive move. By adding more tools that counter various offensive moves from various floor positions, the defender becomes a complete defensive player who can quickly adjust to any new offensive situation.

The first fundamental base that defensive positioning should consider is the position of the ball. Flexible spacing and positioning should also consider all ball movement and position of receivers.

FLOOR POSITIONS

The flexing movements of the defense should arrive just ahead of the ball being caught by your opponent. We use the expression: *"Be on time"* as a law of flexible defense.

Diagram 2-10 illustrates various defense floor positions taken against the ball situated in different floor positions.

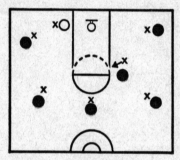

Diagram 2-10

STANCES AND DRILLS

Body mechanics should be considered the first tool to use in successfully defending the opponent. It is the starting base in developing the necessary defense tools to counter many of the offensive patterns.

Players may have balance with legs spread anywhere from shoulder width to extra wide double shoulder width. The best stance for each player depends to a great extent on his physical make-up.

Balance is needed to propel the body with starting speed in any direction. The leg spread is the key ingredient to the success of the shuffle step.

Stance Drills: Flex straight down in a half crouch with the balance on the balls of the feet. Practice breaking away in all directions.

Be sure your upper trunk is in an upright position as you flex. The hands should be down and away from your body with forearms at a slight angle from your elbows, palms up, relaxed and ready to help the pivot or to drive in any direction from the starting position.

Experiment with a lower or higher stance in order to find the best possible stance to give the maximum starting speed in any direction.

Experiment with feet parallel, left foot forward, right foot forward, in your stance-start practice. Use a whistle or use directional pointing as a signal to go.

The coach's goal should be to help each player attain maximum defensive movement.

The foot stance can be too close causing the body to be top heavy in reacting to a fast stop, change of direction, or vertical, lateral, or angle movements at top speed.

Body Position

The extreme double shoulder width stance tends to make a player flat-footed which creates difficulty in starting fast. Instead of shoving against the floor for starting, his wide stance forces him to exaggerate and to lift his body weight before he shoves off on the start. Such a stance will develop a tendency to take large shuffle movements which slow down his start and acceleration. It also produces an up and down movement called shoulder bobbing. This motion wastes energy. It lifts the body weight on each shuffle motion and the feet are off the floor for too long a time.

The extreme double shoulder width stance can be used at court center against dribblers with equal left and right drive ability. The wide stance has some merit when you are playing off a clever dribbler in the non-shooting area.

A defensive player may find himself caught in midair as his opponent changes direction. A shoulder width plus two or three inches outside the shoulder gives the defender the quickest reaction, providing his shuffle footwork is *close* to the floor *at all times*.

His shoulders should be so level a glass of water could stay on his shoulder without a drop being spilled.

The wide stand might serve a purpose for a boxing move-in to trap the offensive player or on a move-in after the dribble stops.

The boxing or belly-up position has come into more use as the offense has used more overhead passes. It is effective against players who do not have fakes or counter pivots, or against those who deliver the ball and then just stand.

Diagram 2-11. One simple defensive drill: set up the offensive dribbler, start out of the corner and have the defender hold the angle position, forcing the dribbler toward the top of the key. With dribbler going away from the basket don't overshift forward. Be alert for reverse dribble to the basket. Keep shoulders down on a level with the dribbler. Keep your two to two-and-a-half foot spacing; crowding will open up a pivot drive to the basket.

If you lose position, release back quickly to try to gain pressure position before the shot goes up.

Diagram 2-12. Pass ball to wing who is feeder to the inside moves. Defender practices moving in fast with the box stance, forcing a quick overhead pass release, or forcing feeder to dribble, thus destroying the timing to the inside. This is a good move against the overhead pass if you change and drop back into the pass lanes on occasion.

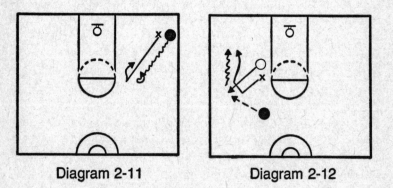

Diagram 2-11   Diagram 2-12

Be sure to stay tight if the passer gets the pass off. Force him to back off or move sideways just as you jump back toward the basket in order to get a good position again. Use the pass lane pressure stance. The feet should have a continuous motion. The inside foot forward is positioned to protect the baseline drive. Keep the body in motion and ready for the inside or baseline dribble.

Perhaps your rule should be to use every possible defensive move against the offense, providing the offense does not have a good counter move. This philosophy should be kept under control or you may be making one mistake for each of many situations, which added together will defeat the purpose of flexibility in defensive positioning.

Stance

A belly-tight defensive stance does intimidate some *inexperienced* players. It works best against teams that want to dribble laterally or on an arc for ball handling purposes. A good ball-handling team will dribble on the angle or move the ball with short passes to create more problems for the defense. Experience has shown that the belly position used on every occasion causes many errors. In a good position stance the defender's belly is protected with a shoulder level crouch stance.

The wide stance seems to be a one-spot defense with a philosophy of all or nothing. It might be used to trap in ten-second corners, baseline corners, and in other two-timing situations depending upon the offensive moves, or in the game areas of closing half-time or closing game time. *Surprise* and careless positioning by the opponents are the most important ingredients for successful traps.

Unless your gambling instincts are strong, it is better to put constant hard pressure on the ball and on the close pass lanes to force the ball movement toward a second defender before two-timing occurs. Players should hope to force the error rather than to make an error that costs two more points that later must be won back. Be aware of overloading the defensive player with an assignment that could not be handled by one particular stance or position.

Quick Start Drills

One drill should have a teammate point out the direction break just as the defender hits the low set of his stance. Body control is enhanced by lowering the center of gravity. The amount of body flex should be gauged according to the best possible *individual* position for starts in any direction. By keeping your upper torso erect the shoulders should be positioned slightly back of your flexed knees. Be sure to check your shoulder position against the height of opponent's shoulders. You should be at least even, or slightly under. This position keeps him away from your middle. You are a defeated defensive player if your position allows the opponent to contact your body.

Diagram 2-13. Defenders O1 and O2 block out offensive players X1 and X2. O3 shoots ball on the board then breaks out to the outlet areas. O1 or O2 gets the rebound and passes to outlet O3 on the side. Passing can be short, medium, or long. As O1 or O2 gains a rebound, X1 and X2 release with fast first steps to get even or ahead of the outlet pass. They may be out in front of the key, or at the ten-second line, or back at the free-throw line. They should get position on their opponents and the ball quickly while going down the court center.

Diagram 2-14. This shows shuffle-step retreat moves with left and right pivots. The first three steps in accelerating are most important. Reverse the shuffle retreat, right and left, several times on the way down court. Use hand and arm to assist the pivot in a quick getaway from the pivot spot.

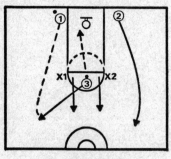

Diagram 2-13

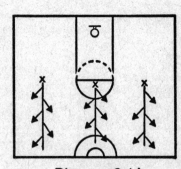

Diagram 2-14

Diagram 2-15. Guards X1 and X2, at the top of the key, pick up the three-man fast break and drop back into a vertical defensive alignment at the head of the key.

Diagram 2-16. Defense men on their own execute the various

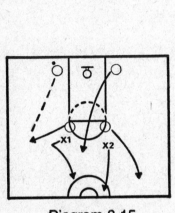

Diagram 2-15

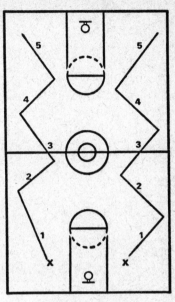

Diagram 2-16

flexible moves that would counter offensive moves. Execute this at game condition speed. This allows over-learning of mechanics without pressure, and serves as a honing up of the defensive tools. Going full court length the defender should execute counter moves against the offensive skills. Follow with pressuring dribble full court.

Shuffle lateral, angle, vertical retreat, advance, banana, release on one-half times full reverses, run for position, sideline trap, faking with hands, change of pace, all these can be executed on the shuffle trip down the floor.

1. First retreat shuffle move, using the left or the right foot forward.
2. Shuffle retreat, turn and run.
3. Shuffle retreat, banana run to pick up position.
4. Shuffle retreat, quick release against change of pace, then gain position.
5. Shuffle retreat, advance quickly, and retreat.

3

Coaching Body Control for
Execution of Flexible Defensive Tools

Body control is the essential prerequisite to successful defensive play. Balance is a key to defense. The offensive players' moves are concentrated on taking away this key.

Each defensive player has an optimum ability to control all his counter moves. Being forced to counter just over his optimum ability, the defender may lose balance or body control.

This optimum of control can be improved during the day-to-day defensive practice by improving strength; by better stance; by more experience in reading offensive moves; by maturation of coordination; and by assuming flexible position that will offset the speed variables of the players.

The greater the number of flexing tools the defender develops, the greater the range of successful defensive play. Flexible defense also increases the number and speed of adjustments that must be available for instant execution by the defender.

Body control may come slowly to some players, especially during sudden growing spurts. However, body control may mature almost overnight. An important factor is constant work for balance.

HAND ACTION SKILLS AND DRILLS

Hand action control is the twin brother of foot control. It helps shuffle positioning, cuts pass lanes, pressures shots, tags passes, forces traveling, forces traps for held balls, and also harrasses offensive moves.

The position of a player's arms and hands is extremely important for efficient defensive play. Overextension of your arms can pull you off balance because your balance and body weight will be pulled too far forward over the knees. The arms fully extended generally dip the shoulders, which brings the body center of gravity over the front foot. This adds a count or two to your start in a new direction.

Have your shoulders relaxed, your hands down, when you are a distance from the basket and the dribbler is out of shooting range. Your hands come up to mirror the ball and the pass lanes as the dribbler gets into shooting range.

Controlled Hand Action

The hand action in pressuring the ball must work separately from the leg action shuffle that keeps you in position. If the upper trunk of the body is not relaxed, the movement will freeze the actions together to create stuttered foot action. This takes away balance and foot speed.

Hand work against the shot should be improved at every opportunity. Poor hand action against the shot costs teams more ball games than other defensive mistakes.

In many school practice sessions I have observed, the coaches do not come up with any drills to obtain maximum pressure without fouling. You cannot call losing games at the free throw line a minor detail, can you?

The first part of the error in pressuring is made by the defender being too far away from the shooter as he starts the shot. A defender's normal reaction is to leap forward and up which makes body contact a surety.

The second part of the error is the failure to keep the arms and hands straight up in front of the shot.

The third part of the error is failure to be in a jump flex before the shot, thus making the defender late with the shot pressure.

The fourth part of the error is to take off too far away from the shooter. Broad jumping allows the defender to make body contact as he tries to pressure the shot.

Diagram 3-1. A good practice drill to eliminate the errors of pressuring the shot: Have the defender approach the shot maker from different angles. Work both the inside-out move to pressure and the outside-in move to pressure. You can use two balls.

Diagram 3-2. Two-ball drill to get defender to move quick to pressure shots. One ball passes from side to key shooter and the other ball passes to the side shooter. Defender number four pressures the shot then hurries back out to pressure the side shot.

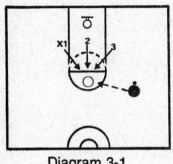

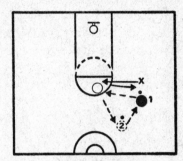

| Diagram 3-1 | Diagram 3-2 |

The defender's arms and hands should be in a medium position if opponent is within shooting range. This gives defender an opportunity to move his hands up or down the shortest distance to pressure the ball. Usually one arm will be up and the other down when defending a dribbler or passer within shooting distance. *Never* allow your extended arms to pull your weight balance forward over the knees. Again this slows down your reaction time.

By keeping hand pressure on the ball you have developed a very important tool. *To mirror the ball* you place the hands in front of the ball and move hands with each change in the ball's position. Remember the palms are curved, facing inside or up, in order to strike without catching the arms of your opponent.

Drill Statement. The drills 3-3 through 3-18 are considered in sequence of usage after the skill is learned. The sequence might change according to the past skill experiences of your players.

Diagram 3-3. A good practice drill is to shuffle step at speed while executing various defensive moves with arms working and darting to pressure ball. If hand pressures force the opponent to expose the ball against dribbler, make a hand flick to tag it. Remember the shuffle step should increase in speed as hand flick is used. Offensive player steps in several directions to force defender to shuffle feet up and back, left and right.

Diagram 3-4. Hand-to-hand tag drill used to develop hand control, hand quickness, and hand fakes. Move feet with upper body perfectly relaxed. Contest most number of tags in two minutes, alternating starts.

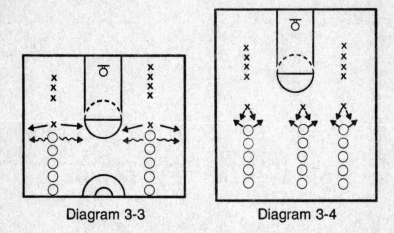

Diagram 3-3   Diagram 3-4

Diagram 3-5. This drill teaches the defender to mirror the ball at all times. Follow the offensive man with shuffle step. He makes one or two dribbles using a front cross dribble on occasion to force hand and foot change by defender.

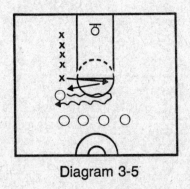

Diagram 3-5

Diagram 3-6. Drill has offensive man using one or two dribbles using a change of pace. Defender must keep inside hand pointed at dribbler's inside hip. Work on two-dribble vertical advance and retreat moves.

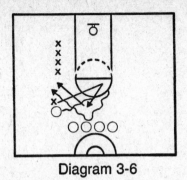

Diagram 3-6

LEG STRENGTH FOR GREATER DEFENSIVE RANGE

Proper body stance with balance allows leg strength to produce top efficiency in starting speed, in stops, in body control, and in directional changes.

Leg strength can be developed faster by using special drills such as speed weight lifting, multiple jumping in rebounding, jump stops at end of fast movement, Jumping Jack drill working for high lift, push-and-pull wrestling, jumping backward, and jumping on the four corners of a three-foot square.

Players with great leg strength can develop a greater range of defense tools and positions. And they can take on extra overload assignments.

Overloading in defense means to assume over-playing positions to stop an individual opponent with recovery ability, or to work defense beyond his normal game assignment; to drop in to harrass inside post play; to two-time ball if your man is moving away from the basket or when opponent is standing still beyond his shot percentage areas. Or you may be given a free rein to intercept passes and to mess up the opposition's patterns.

LEG STRENGTH FOR BALANCE AND STOPS

Leg strength efficiency depends upon how well the body is in balance with the weight carried on the balls of the feet. We should state again that the starting motion develops from the floor thrust off the inside of the foot, finishing the thrust off the great toe. The details of the stance and motion action which uses a foot spread slightly wider than the shoulders must be understood.

Body balance in the shuffle move is held between the feet until you have the true direction that must be covered by your defensive move. Shuffle explanations will come from time to time in specific defense areas.

The swinging motion of the body's center of gravity should be in *constant action*. The feet should *never* be allowed to heel down and stop even if the opponent stops. With the body alive at all times it is possible to break into a fast shuffle or to run more quickly in any direction.

Remember the old saying: "Take away the defender's balance and you have destroyed his ability to guard."

LEG STRENGTH FOR JUMP-STOP CONTROL

Leg strength is most important to execute balanced steps. Balance is the key to successfully countering offensive moves. The stride stop and the one-count jump-stop are the two stops with general use. The stride stop applies pressure control on one foot at a time. It is a slower stop motion that allows the defender to recover his balance or in reverse allows the offensive man more room to operate his skills and passes. You do this stride stop most of the time when you are running on defense.

The one-count jump-stop uses the power of both legs to stop your body from a fast move. Yet it gives balance to explode again in any direction the offense player takes. By stopping in the right position with balance you have some control over many of your opponent's moves and this places you in the role of a dictating defender.

The one-count jump-stop is the best tool against talented mobile offensive men. It expands your mobility after a stop and allows you a continuation or a quick direction change. It plays a key role while staying on time with changes of speed and changes in direction. You have greater thrust to start your body moving after stops.

DRILLS FOR SPEED AND CONTROL

The following drills are used to develop the basic moves that will counter individual offensive moves.

By learning offensive moves you gain greater insight into countering the moves defensively.

Diagram 3-7. Offense forward-reverse pivot drill without ball. Defender moves forward and puts pressure on pivoter. One-count jump-stops. Defender approaches from straight on, left and right sides, and counters with shuffle jump stop. Force pivot to turn inside and outside.

Diagram 3-8. Dribble drill with front cross to side. Defender forces pivot or cross over to close sideline and counter dribble with spacing and position.

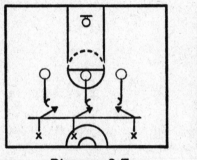 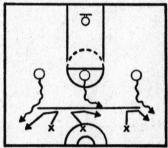

Diagram 3-7   Diagram 3-8

Diagram 3-9. Defender X1 has a ballside position against wing O1 starting at low post. The defender's position has shut off the straight move to high post. X1 must pressure hard with the inside hand pressuring possible pass lane. As X1 passes the half-way mark toward the sideline, the space between the players should increase. The postioning is a little toward the ball with the inside

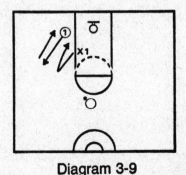

Diagram 3-9

hand still pressuring the possible pass lane. This positioning is detail but essential in case O1 reverses and goes backdoor.

Diagram 3-10. This drills the perimeter guard X1 into releasing toward the ball and the basket. It will keep X1 ballside all the way to the low post position. O1 may counter by cutting down inside of the screen. X1 will still take the same ballside lane and front O1 at the low post.

Diagram 3-11. X1 maintains a ballside position as O1 tries to open a pass lane by moving toward the sideline. O1 reverses and goes back through the key. X1 must move into his running lane to get by a possible screen to maintain a high ballside position on the baseline. X1 never takes his eyes off O1. By turning his head toward the ball, X1 can see O1 and the ball, while his ballside hand is pressuring a possible pass lane.

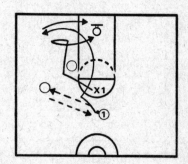

Diagram 3-10   Diagram 3-11

These drills apply learned spacing and position knowledge and movement to one-on-one assignment going full court. Each drill emphasizes specific offensive techniques that must be successfully countered. From the early still drills used to develop the mechanics of the defender's tools, we come to drills 12 to 18 that put the tools to work against full court pressure.

Diagram 3-12. Work one-on-one without ball full court. Defender keeps driving dribbler toward sidelines. Turn his drive to center of court, back and to sidelines. Full court shuffle maintaining position and spacing with quick release and attack on each direction change.

Diagram 3-13. Dribblers use change of pace, fake turns, reverses and front cross-in dribbling. Put in some whistle stops. Be sure to concentrate on spacing and positioning. $\backsim$ = dribble path.

Diagram 3-14. Banana drill to recover loss of position with shuffle-run-shuffle moves. The banana tool is used after loss of position. Defender releases toward basket, gets ahead and positions to pressure again.

Diagram 3-15. From shuffle to run. Pivot on balls of both feet. Against a fast dribble, shuffle may not keep up. Turn, run for position and shuffle. May drill first without dribbler.

This is game condition effort.

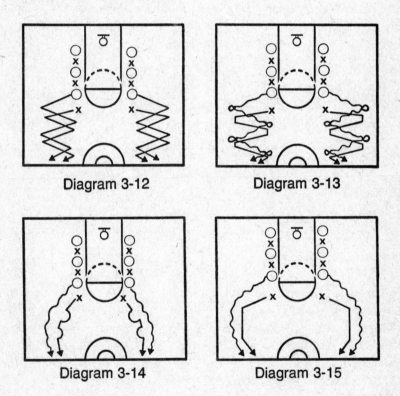

Diagram 3-12   Diagram 3-13

Diagram 3-14   Diagram 3-15

The following drills will increase the learning skills given in the last chapter. Several of these new drills will give opportunities to practice a particular counter skill. The use of different drills will keep interest high and eliminate boredom caused by the use of the same drill day after day.

A key to great defensive play is body control balance. Every situation has floor positions for the offensive player. Each of these drills will offer a specific counter move to control the offensive situation.

After the skills are well learned these drills will offer ways to counter offensive penetration attempts. But be sure the problems are set up in the exact position on the floor that most patterns use.

The following drills will add more situations to help the defender to develop greater position, spacing, and movement skills.

Diagram 3-16. A shuffle speed drill for footwork, foot-hand coordination, conditioning, hustle, and the practicing of all shuffle moves. When making the 5 to 6 move (as given on the diagram) great emphasis should be put on retreat, advance, stops, change of direction, talk, and extra burst of speed.

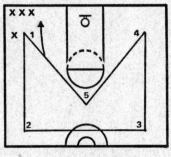

Diagram 3-16

Shuffle action 1 to 2—retreat and advance. 2 to 3—fast lateral mixed with one count stops and direction changes. 3 to 4—again advance, retreat. Add fast hand action correlated with footwork. Start your offense-defense philosophy with Talk! Talk! Talk! 4 to 5—taking opponent out of the corner. Imagine you are not letting opponent reverse on you or beating you over the top. 5 to 6—break your opponent to sideline away from the basket. Don't allow him to come back. Talk! Talk! Talk!

Diagram 3-17. Use a four-foot length of yarn and tie one end to the belt of an offensive man. Then tie the other end to the belt of a defensive man. It is fun to see whether the offensive man can break the yarn when working lateral shuffle skills and advance-retreat shuffles. This drill increases action speed, concentration, body relaxation, balance, and confidence. It also develops greater defense condition. Try lateral movements first, then try vertical movements.

Diagram 3-18. O1 and O2 play catch. X3 defender fronts offense opponent O3 and shuffles with arm in pass lane. Shuffles, turns his head to see the ball as he passes center of the key. You may use this drill with the defender using an open shuffle stance facing the ball. Compare results of both moves to find the best flexing tool.

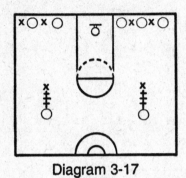 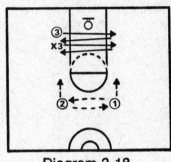

Diagram 3-17   Diagram 3-18

TIMED POSITION AS PASS COMES IN

Assume that the defensive player is in position at the time the ball hits the offensive player's hands, has a position to force movement, and pressures passes.

If the player fails to be in position as his opponent receives the ball, the player is forced to shuffle-advance toward him. The player must fake moves into pressuring the shot and be ready for the drive. This late positioning places the defensive player in the weakest possible position. The defensive player's motto during the game should be: "Come to me!"

By forcing the opponent into continuous motion, you are using what is considered to be master defensive play.

If a player is forced out of his shuffle to run against speedy players, he must be sure to pivot on the balls of both feet while shifting from shuffle to run.

Defenders should be ready to learn the variables to aid them in defending various floor positions. Drills will emphasize multiple learning opportunities to develop the important defensive footwork.

Variety of situations is the spice that prevents boredom in defensive learning. After defender stops opponent on sidelines, he must be ready to quickly release his position pressure in case opponent slows down, fakes reverse back or front, or executes front or back reverse. Then he must go back in with pressure from his new front position. *This is one of the great defensive secrets.* When, or if, you teach the defender to apply pressure without teaching him the recovery skill, you give him a one-shot pressure tool.

A quick drop-off release toward the basket, at any sign of a true move by opponent, is the essence of good defensive play.

4

Individual Flexible Defense Correlated with Team Units

The importance of defense should not be underestimated. What do you do on poor shooting nights? You put on a tough defense to give you an opportunity to win a low scoring game. The opposition, when it knows its special shot areas are being pressured, can wilt.

INDIVIDUAL AND TEAM
DEFENSE PROBLEMS AND DRILLS

Remember that tough defense creates a positive psychological attitude for the defending team when it goes to offense. The pressure on scoring baskets diminishes greatly when your defense makes the opposition pay dearly for attempting to get the two points back.

The preparing and perfecting of individual flexible man-to-man press skills is the key to success.

Here are some answers to the problems that face each individual player. Remember the *quick release* move gives the player time to counter the offensive man's true move. At the moment of release your defense pressure is off, but when position is gained the pressure is back on again. Defense should aim its pressure ahead of this moving target's real move, just as you would aim a shot ahead of flying ducks.

Defense is played *by the inch* in shifts of positions with *enough flexing inches* to shut off the opponent's attack. If the defensive man allows the offensive man to fake him into exaggerating his counter move, the offensive man's next move will give him the position he needs to combat the defensive pressure.

A player's aggressive offensive-defensive pressures tell his opponent what direction he can go. Don't allow the offense to dictate the movement.

Playing pressure flexible defense out on the 30-foot perimeter calls for great concentration and mental discipline to maintain the proper spacing. *Never overplay a direction change.* Concentrate on every move toward the right hand, always force your opponent down the sidelines, and never allow him to come back into the middle. This is the play against the right-handed dribbler. Just the opposite for a left-handed dribbler. If he executes well in both directions, shut off the right-hand because it will beat you three out of five times.

The Flexible Boxing Tool

Boxing is moving in tight with parallel feet and with hands up. This is considered your boxing defensive tool. Be sure you teach the defender the jump-back release toward the basket before he tries to pressure the man and the pass lane. If the defender is caught going in as the ball is released he should force opponent to step back or move sideways before he can move to the basket. At the instant opponent passes, *at his first move*, defender should execute his jump-back release and go for position.

The defender should learn to defend the overhead pass without losing his assignment. He may alternate, or work the stepping back, with hands up against the possible pass to the inside posts. Especially if passer is out of good shooting range.

In blocking off in key near basket, *defender uses one hand up instead of two*. The defender will be in a better position to jump and pressure shot or pass. First, the defender should not give his assignment much time to pass. Make him pass or move immediately. If defender uses a surprise drop-off, he should be sure to be in the passing lane position to the inside posts. Second, the defender should be alert for pivoting, or moving skill, of opponent who holds ball high for overhead pass.

Don't forget the moves that a dribbler uses to constantly close defense's operating space. A continuous moving adjustment should be made in order to maintain good position.

If the defender feels a loss of inches in his spacing, he should release toward the center of court and basket, then drive to get ahead, and attack from good position again. Call this *executing the banana move*.

How many times have you seen a defensive player run along the side of a dribbler? Invariably he gets sucked in and fouls, or puts no pressure on the advance of the ball. But if the defensive player maintains a *forcing, angling position* with enough front pressure to keep the dribbler from going to the baseline, he has what can be considered *excellent defensive play position*.

The following pick-up drills are fundamental keys to develop flexible team defense. The time to put pressure on the team playing the ball inbounds, or picking up at the ten second line, is at the beginning of the plays. By putting pressure and position on the pass receiver as the ball comes in, you force him to watch the ball without much vision of his teammates.

Diagram 4-1. Drill the one-on-one full court. This teaches court pick-up and pressuring of opponent. If you overplay toward ball, you should be alert for the long pass. If your assignment comes back for pass, be sure you have position to force him toward sideline as ball hits his hands. This is *pressuring the inbound pass*.

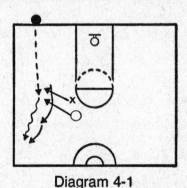

Diagram 4-1

Diagram 4-2. This is similar to the first drill but adds the speed catch-up move to the defender's flexible tools. If defender loses a perfect position momentarily in pressuring the dribbler, he should release away and down ahead of the dribbler. His speed will allow him to regain a pressure position.

Diagram 4-3. This is the *basic ten-second pick-up defense*. The

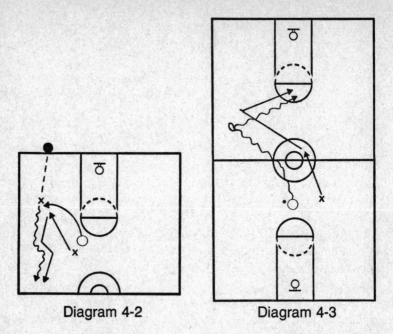

Diagram 4-2   Diagram 4-3

perfection of these defensive tools will further harass the offensive patterns and *keep the offensive man moving* through his good shot areas. This is important. By pushing out, the defender lengthens the pass lanes and thus disturbs the offensive timing. He creates a better chance to intercept a pass. This also puts extra pressure on the passer. This drill teaches the defender how to drop off and wait for the opponent to approach. He must be sure to give ground slowly, faking and forcing the dribbler to the sideline. The defender is cutting one-third to one-half of the court off from his defensive assignment. He should not get caught standing still. As the opponent approaches, he should pick up slowly and be ready for a change of speed and force his opponent to the sidelines.

ATTACKING OFFENSE PRESSURES
WITH FLEXIBLE DEFENSE

Full pressure consists of occupying the player's mind, handicapping his full vision, giving him one known path for his move. More pressure may be added by forcing him to work harder than his normal tempo, by mirroring the ball from the inside pass lanes, and by forcing him to the sidelines if this move is part of your team defense. Pressure him more by keeping him on the move, especially when he tries to get to his shooting spots. One of the most important pressure flexes possible would be to gain position before the ball hits the opponent's hands, thereby giving him just one alternative which is to move the ball in the direction you give him. This tool will be emphasized again and again in special floor situations.

DEFENSE AGAINST THE DRIBBLER

Many coaches want the playmaker to come down the middle and drive for a shot or pass off. Your flexible counter should take away the center move drive and force dribbler to either side. And keep him there.

By being on time all during the game you force him away from his shot areas and cut down on his passing and receiving passes. You also make him play from his weakness.

Perimeter pressure is the most difficult to maintain with real consistency. It takes a determined will to continue the same pressure and add a little more after you have lost him once or twice. After an opponent beats a defender his confidence rises about one hundred percent.

Doubts will creep into your player's mind unless he is a tough-minded player who loves a challenge and comes up with greater pressure. This kind of play is a tremendous challenge for the defender.

The several defensive floor positions on man-and-ball will be considered as independent game situations for the sake of clarity.

Full Court Flexible Positioning

The first man-to-man defense floor position to be considered is the full court coverage problems and the tools used to control the offensive moves.

In an early drill let the pass get inbound. The defender moves with the pass-in on ball receiver from a center inside position. This position gives the offensive dribbler just the sideline move. Remember the defender should be near the receiver whom he will pick up and pressure. The defender should start with his opponent rather than after the opponent picks up momentum and catches defender coming in. The main objective is to eliminate the straight-line down-court move by the offensive player. Right hand dribblers should be forced to their weakest move. Consider too the strength of attack on either side of the offense. Again, spacing position and intense concentration are all-important tools that must be used efficiently to be successful. Once the dribbler is started on the angle, never let him get off the lane left open to him.

You should *teach continuous intense concentration as a must,* if your defense is going to be successful. *Keep your players in guiding and fronting positions which include correct spacing* to eliminate problems. The inside hand next to the dribbler should be the correct position to pressure front crossovers. While the outside hand presses the dribbler, the inside hand should be pointing at the opponent's inside hip when he is on the angle moving toward the sideline.

Diagram 4-4. From the center of the court to about one-half the distance toward the sideline, the defensive position is almost a front position. Player should not over-shift beyond a front ball position at this point on the floor. Moving from this point toward the sideline, the position changes gradually to the center of the opponent's body, then moves forward to the outside shoulder position of the opponent as he nears the sidelines. The defender should be mentally ready for a change of pace to drive down the sideline, or reverse back inside. *The fault of most players is over-shifting when going to the sideline,* thus allowing the opponents to beat him back inside.

The sideline is on the defender's side. Use it! Do not make a sideline out of your position.

Diagram 4-5. For defending the lateral dribbler from left to right, the defender needs intensity of concentration to keep position on the ball. He should never lose position. He should be ready for a stop, go, and change of pace. When O1 gets past the center of the court the defender should be ready for the turn down. He should force him on the angle and keep him on it. O1 reverses, then X1 takes away his number one objective. The instant the reverse starts, X1 should release and gain back position to pressure again.

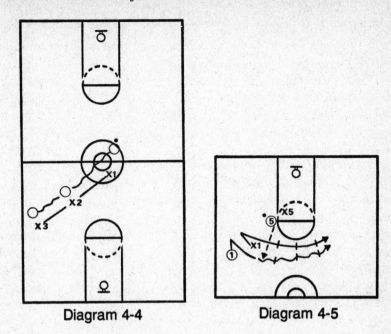

Diagram 4-4   Diagram 4-5

Diagram 4-6. This defensive play can be used against a good dribbler. X2 takes a side position to allow O1 to dribble down the sideline. He follows until X1 picks up O1, pinning O1 against the sideline near the ten-second line. X2 follows down ready to pick up his assignment as O2 moves down court.

Diagram 4-7. The dribbler should make one of the following moves: Try to execute a change of pace and continue down the sidelines, or, try his reverse move with a pivot or behind-the-back dribble. *The defender's release back is very important*. It should be

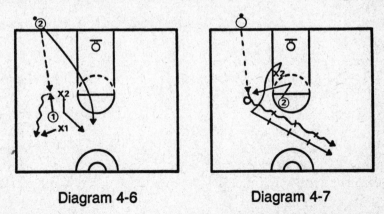

Diagram 4-6   Diagram 4-7

quick and deep enough to give the defender an angle shot at picking O2 up again before he gets to the key. Ten to sixteen inches
might be enough, according to the speed of the opponent.

Don't forget that the closing action to gain pressure position
again should be aimed well ahead of the moving opponent. The
release spacing is in addition to the normal 3 to 4 feet. The spacing
varies according to the speed difference between offensive and
defensive player. *Emphasize* over and over *that spacing is based on
the dribbler's speed and the diminishing size of the court*. Full
effort should be used to challenge the dribbler at all times. *Defensive players should close in every inch possible without losing position*. This kind of defensive effort will begin to occupy the offensive
dribbler's mind and give him less opportunity to keep in contact
with his team's thinking and action.

The flexible man-to-man team pressure will have an important
condition advantage necessary to keep both offense and defense
skills at a high degree of efficiency throughout the whole game.

Pressure play tends to force opponents to a tempo higher or
faster than their normal pace. This will tire them during different
parts of the game—especially the taller players. The tiring team
will shorten its shots and lose concentration which will make for
more turnovers.

SPACE RELATIONSHIPS IN FULL COURT
AND IN TEN-SECOND AND QUARTER DEFENSES

The final and most difficult step is to bring the five defenders
together into a unified pressure action to hold assignment, go for
passes, and be ever alert to make help moves against the ball
movement.

Spacing against opponents is critical. The defenders are covering
full court with advantage going to the offense. The deep defenders
should have ballside position just enough to contest pass but not far
enough to allow opponent to break back for the open long pass.

All offense fake motions should be covered without committing
oneself until the offense shows its true move. Read the offense
set-up and anticipate possible pass lanes.

Be offensive-defensive minded. We might make a space rule that the offensive player must not get the advantage of a completed pass in a 20-foot drive effort. Once you are back defending the dangerous shooting areas, some general spacing rules can be made:

Space Distances

Inside the key area the defensive man should be approximately 12 to 14 inches away in spacing; from the 18 to 22 foot area he can use 2½ to 3½ feet; and from 23 to 28 feet he can use 3 to 3½ feet spacing. All this is subject to changes according to adjustments for speed, screens, and other matching variables. Guarding away from the ball is a distinct problem for most players. It will be discussed under a separate heading. Other variables may arise from the teaming up with teammates to stop ball penetration. All players should recognize some responsibility to stop or to slow down dribbler by the ten second line.

The ability to pressure full court gives a distinct advantage in tight or come-from-behind games. It will cut down some of the taller teams' advantage on the boards. Against inexperienced teams it forces passing errors and creates havoc in their patterns. Expanded defense forces passing lanes to be extended and interferes with positioning of players.

Diagram 4-8. This illustrates space relationship between the offense and the defender, along with team moves to pressure close pass lanes. Full court variations will be considered in Chapter 6.

X1 should position and pressure pass lanes of the close offensive pass receiver and concentrate on ballside position on O1 as he breaks in for return pass.

X2 should concentrate hard to contest the short pass lanes of O2.

X3 should have a step on O3 toward ball position against a center of court break, and a close ball-trailing position if O3 breaks to basket.

X4 should eliminate O4 from getting a pass lane moving toward the ball and have ballside position against O4 if he breaks to middle.

X5 should cover all long passes and be fearless about going for the passes. He is a safety valve against any break offensive player. He can fade with his O5 opponent but play loose for long passes and not lose middle position until after pass starts.

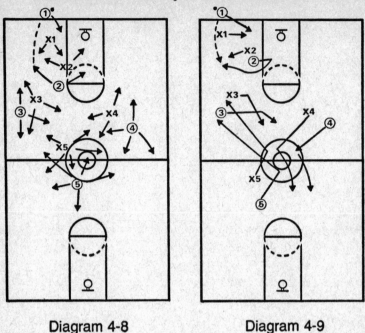

Diagram 4-8   Diagram 4-9

Team tools should cover the three close-pass lanes like a blanket. Defenders should be alert to help from the side and cover back on their assignments. Strategy is to force the ball to the sideline and force the dribbler to move close to his teammate allowing a two-time to happen, slide screen moves or over the top, and stay on the assignment. Defenders should keep the team pressure on, force errors, and be alert to aid in slowing down the dribbler. Talk! Talk! Talk! X5 acts as a quarterback.

Diagram 4-9. The defender closes in on close pass lanes to ball after first pass comes in to player No. 2. The arrows of both offense and defense show the direction of breaks to shake off defensive pressure and to start the ball up court. Pushing your defense down court to start pressure at the three quarter area places great responsibility on each player. You should check carefully your team's endurance and speed. One weak link spells defeat. This move on defense changes the game tempo, pressures offense to change, and adds confusion to offense while it is trying to set up pattern.

5

Synchronizing
Flexible Defensive Players

Synchronizing defensive players with space and positioning de-
tails to tie the defenders into unified action to counter offensive
moves—this is our flexible goal.

SPACE: THE KEY TO FLEXIBLE DEFENSE

Spacing has been mentioned earlier in relationship to other
tools, but because of its importance it requires individual treat-
ment.

Most players understand spacing to mean the distance between
their position and their opponent's position, but the number one
objective *in spacing* is to *keep a successful counter position against*
the ball.

Speed relationship between the two players *is a factor in a space*
flexing consideration.

Pattern types of offense that include screening should be recog-
nized by proper spacing and counter-positioning on the floor. The
ball movement and position should be added to the counter flexing
of this space tool.

Good spacing judgment, combined with position and concentra-
tion, creates pressure that eliminates or hampers the moves of the
offensive player. Don't forget the value of *full vision* in making the
right move to counter the offense.

The spacing and position of a player must be on time before the
ball hits the opponent's hands. The *player should be balanced* and
ready to force the ball in a given direction in defensing post play.

Basketball is a unique game with the center as the hub of the four man square. *The center is the key to defensive and offensive boards.*

The best defense against the post patterns is to keep the ball from getting into the pivot post's hands and to force him from the key, which could eliminate a high percentage shooting offense.

POST DEFENSIVE PLAY

All defensive patterns should try to *make it difficult for the offense to be on time* when going down to low post or coming up to high post. The biggest mistakes made against patterns are the failures to fall off with release toward the ball when away from the ball, and to have ballside position when near the ball. Remember to have a good release toward the ballside on the single, double, and triple key posts that sit across the key from the passer. Be sure to be in the pass lane to the ball with feet constantly moving. *Position above the posts ballside. Keep in motion and watch man and ball MOVEMENT.*

Diagram 5-1. This shows the relationship of defender X2 to his opponent and the *spacing release* necessary to counter all moves over the top or back door. He should eliminate the pass lane to the ball with his flexible positioning and spacing. X1 spaces to keep O1 from driving baseline or coming over the top of key. He pressures pass lanes with his hands, always ready for a give-and-go play. Many times X2 fails to counter by moving inch for inch with his man, but gets burned by allowing the opponent to take away some of the spacing distance.

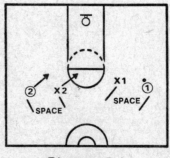

Diagram 5-1

Diagram 5-2. This shows X2 on opponent with ball on the pass. He releases toward basket and back toward ball to create enough spacing to counter the break potential of O2. He should spread vision to cover both assignment and ball. If he does not it is impossible for him to cover the pass lane when O1 moves ball before passing. X2 maintains ballside position all the way to the basket.

The next three diagrams show position and spacing against three inside post moves. *Spacing* in this crucial shooting area must be *by the inch*. To play the pass lanes on post moves is just one phase of the problem. If too loose, opponent fades for high under-the-basket pass. If too tight he pivots away free for a pass.

Diagram 5-3. Shows position of X2 against inside post O2. The team play of this situation would be: X1 drops back in pass lane and is alert for a baseline drive. X2 should be alert for O2 who could execute a quick fade toward basket and come back. *A good post man will not stay if the pass lane is taken away.*

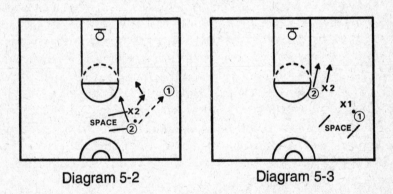

Diagram 5-2   Diagram 5-3

Diagram 5-4. Shows the post O2 faking the high post position going down fast to low post position. X2 should have proper spacing and position against O2 and pass lane before he starts. X2 should beat his opponent going up and keep the pass lane covered. X2 should not allow O2 to go over the top to ball and be ready to cover pass lane all the way to low post. Force him away from basket.

Diagram 5-5. As wing O3 passes back to playmaker O1 team spacing and positioning should be immediately made. X3 releases back quickly, ready for over-the-top or a backdoor move. X1 must move to position in balance as ball hits O1's hands. Team play calls

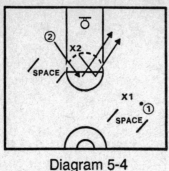

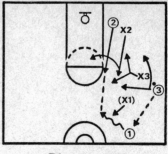

| Diagram 5-4 | Diagram 5-5 |

for X2 to come up with post to cover ballside pass lane. If pass is going to be handled, X2 should quickly jump to position and force ball toward his two teammates.

To take away and contest the passing lanes at all times is the major objective of flexible defensive play.

Post defense positions should be guided by the ball movement and the player positions.

Defensive philosophy should include the role of the offense-defense attitude in pressing the defense attack on the ball and the man. This aggressive move by the defense goes far beyond just countering the attack. *Take away his best move to the ball. Allow only one move available to shut off.*

Floor positions and spacing are based on the offensive player's position in relationship to ball, basket, and his teammates. This position must also recognize the special abilities of each player. *Emphasize the player attributes of flexibility, quickness in a small area, and continuous adjustment to changing situations.*

A player should never stop his body motion completely especially when opponent stops. Confuse offensive timing by keeping in motion. Fake at different run and pass lanes according to ball position.

Diagram 5-6. This shows the position and spacing against the post stack with ball away. Defenders have released toward the ball and positioned high on each post. This forces their opponents to move down with defenders maintaining ballside position. Don't allow stack players to cut over the top for ball. Concentrate on keeping ballside.

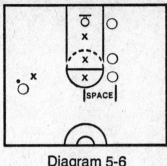

Diagram 5-6

Diagram 5-7. With ball moving toward top of key, defenders should close the spacing to 12 or 14 inches with defender of top post cutting off the pass lane completely. Positioning against lower posts is still high.

Diagram 5-8. The spacing distances should be considered general positions that can be altered to take care of many variables found in individual offensive play. Considering all the variables

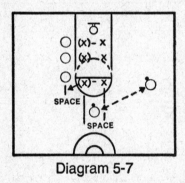

Diagram 5-7

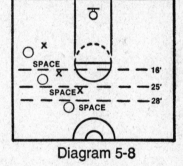

Diagram 5-8

involved in spacing at various distances from the basket, you should consider a general space distance at the start. Later on refine the particular spacing for each individual player at various distances according to his capabilities and his opponent's tools. In the last diagram a spacing of 2 to 2½ feet at the 16 foot distance, 3 feet at the 25 foot distance, and 3½ feet at the 28 foot distance gives the defender the challenge spacing that should promote the desired pressure.

PERIMETER DEFENSE
WITH MOVING TEAM RELATIONSHIPS

Defensive play can be played passively on the perimeter by dropping into a tight key defense providing the perimeter shooting is not good. Or it can be expanded to pressure and harass the playmakers from getting an easy opportunity to set and time their plays.

The first part of team defense pressure is guard-on-guard pressure to keep the passer off balance so he is not in a position to pass accurately to inside receivers. At the same time the inside defenders should pressure and close the ball pass lanes. Perimeter pressure can develop to the point where passes inside are not accurate according to the position of the inside receiver. This causes passes to be tagged or flecked to a sinking teammate as the ball comes inside. The ball-handling guards are the quarterbacks of the pattern. Some teams have a superior playmaker using the second guard as a safety valve.

Diagram 5-9. Defender X1 should hold angle position on dribbler after he turns toward sidelines. At pass to O3, X1 instantly releases back and maintains ball position all the way to low post, through key, easing to sink (or ball position) to the baseline, or to corner if O1 turns out. X2 sinks to front of high post ready to help, or takes his opponent down or over the high post screen and then down. X4 releases to key with ball vision and man ready to take him under the basket, or toward the ball, maintaining ball position. X5 has ball position against high post opponent. If O3 attempts to dribble over post, O5 will pivot into his lane to stop him, then roll to the basket in the lane O5 wants the pass to come.

Diagram 5-10. This shows a three position move on the part of all five players as the ball moves between three offensive players. Hands should be ready to cover right hand dribble or pass. All defenders have inside ballside positions closing to the key and leading their assignments to the ball. The same inside drops would be executed if the assignments failed to stop the ball.

The guard your players defend against may be a good outside shot, a hard driver, and a passing expert all rolled into one. For this reason your inside *defense must be letter perfect in team position-*

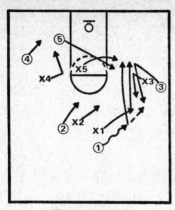

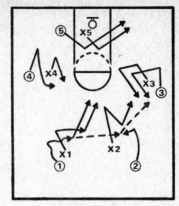

Diagram 5-9   Diagram 5-10

ing ballside on at least the three close pass lanes. All players should
recognize how *important* it is *not to allow an easy pass-in on the
ballside.*

Your use of this style of defense should be based on opponent's
patterns, player skills in relationship to your matching up, equal or
superior inside speed, and height and shooting considerations.
Flexible defense positionings will improve your team's ability to
confine the attack to the opponent's weakest side.

Remember it is folly to use up extra energy to force the offense-
swing to weak side and then give their strong side right back by one
careless move, or the failure of one player. This allows them to get
back to a strong side scoring position.

The guards against the playmakers establish the first perimeter
defense by getting the position, then pressuring to guide opponent's to the side horizontally or on an angle.

The defender should concentrate and fight the dribbler every
inch of the way, putting on more pressure to keep opponent from
going to the baseline with the ball. Remember the tool. Once you
start the dribbler hold him on the angle. Never let him get off.

Diagram 5-11. Offense man starts his move on an arc to draw
defender toward him and to get defender to stay on the arc all the
way which makes defender look weak. *Never, never arc your defense counter moves.* Make small straight line-cuts across the arc
forcing opponent to change again. Continue this move until he
quits moving down or goes out of bounds. You might call this move

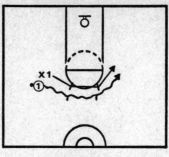

Diagram 5-11

Short Line Cut Releases. Too much cannot be said about how important constant releases and adjustments are in maintaining perfect defense pressure that blunts the attacks.

Diagram 5-12. The defender X1 is working his shuffle moves on short, straight lines. If the defender overplays the ball dribble position, the dribbler will shoot a stop reverse shot in 70 percent area. X1 should remember to shift position to the shooter's hand side. This will block his going to the right for rebound. X1 should be ready for dribbler's quick down or reverse drive as he moves up toward top of key. X1 should not suck in tight at top of the key.

Diagram 5-13. If your one-count stop is synchronized with opponent's stop, be sure to make the quick move to the shooter's shooting hand to put on pressure without fouling. Be sure to front the ball position only on the lateral dribble. Your spacing and position at center of court should be on ball in order to keep position on quick change of pace. You will have more time to release and position on the reverse skill of your opponent.

Diagram 5-12

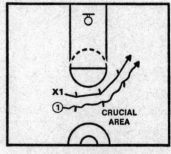

Diagram 5-13

COUNTERING GIVE-AND-GO MOVES
WITH FLEXIBLE DEFENSE

The most dangerous man on the floor is the passer. The simple give-and-go on left or right side court is one of the most effective plays in basketball. The defensive habit, to counter with, is a quick jump-back release deep toward basket and *ballside.* If the passer goes away *be aware of two motions*:

One, a continued right side movement toward the basket countered by having the defender follow him down with approximately a 2½ foot spacing, head turned over right shoulder, left hand up all the way to low post. Expect a stop-and-come-back as you near low post. Make him turn back up on your inside to post so his right dribble to basket is cut off. Be ready before the ball hits his hands.

Two, be aware of his move to lead you away from the ball using a horizontal lane, if possible, then suddenly reversing and cutting hard toward the basket. In trailing him away from the ball remember that this reverse move will come before he reaches the key. After that look for the quick break toward the basket, back across the key, and down as he tries to get pass position. Or look for a loop pass over you. If the cutter goes down the key to low post ballside, stay ballside with spacing to cut off his low post move.

The teammate guarding the passer should be quick to put on baseline pressure and force movement from the passer. This skill or tool can be used against the dribble to wing hand-off and on the breakaway move by the dribbler or wing receiver.

Some defenders force the dribbler to turn his back with dribble for ball protection and stay-in, which is the best way to lose complete control of the situation. *It is very important after turning the dribbler to release back a few inches and expect him to go in either direction.* If you need to outsmart him fake a move in on one side and quickly move to the opposite side for position to flick the ball away.

Diagram 5-14. This pictures how the forward hand-off play to the guard can break, and gives the defense moves used in countering the three O2 moves. At the forward break, X2 defender should trail slightly off of O2's inside shoulder. This eliminates losing the ball position if O2 stops, turns left toward the key to post, or fakes down then turns right to a post position.

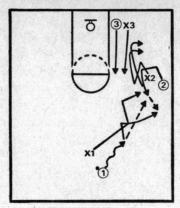

Diagram 5-14

Diagram 5-15. O2 on the second move wants defender to trail behind or on the outside shoulder to make good his key reverse pivot drive to the basket. Defender X2 stays inside shoulder and looks over outside shoulder for the ball.

Diagram 5-16. Move three is the surprise loop pass to the weakside low post position. At the point of turn-down, or through the key, X2 looks over his inside shoulder for a loop pass. He should be within 2 to 2½ feet of the receiver, and increase his speed as he goes over the screen. He goes to the far corner of the basket for a board position or for a pass interception. X2 should have a position high enough on the screen to go over the top to look over his inside

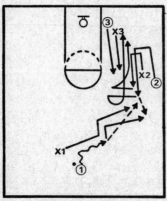

Diagram 5-15

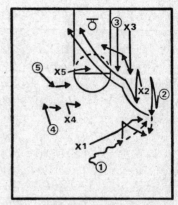

Diagram 5-16

shoulder for the ball. He should not anticipate the reverse drive to the basket. X2 will be late going over the screen. Help should come from a weak-side drop-in by the defense.

Diagram 5-17. This shows wing O1 to post pass, with wing fake over and reverse as a give-and-go. X2 should not overplay position going away from the basket. X2 keeps ballside position to pressure pass. X1 should be careful not to overplay opponent's dribbling up, but pressure pass lane and look for a reverse.

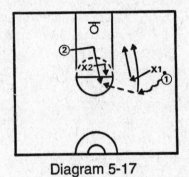

Diagram 5-17

Diagram 5-18. Wing O2 fakes down and comes back for a pass from guard O1. The specific play is the give-and-go, if open, or guard O1 to post for a give-and-go to O2 wing. Post O3 moves out to clear the key for the play to develop. X1, the guard defender,

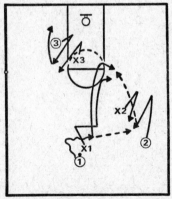

Diagram 5-18

should keep a ballside position all the way. When O1 passes, X1 should execute a quick drop release toward the basket and the ball, and when defending inside the key, play the ball pass lane position hard. The distance to the basket is a little short for an overhead pass to hit. Remember X2 should not overshoot his defense if O2 takes the dribble after faking a pass.

Diagram 5-19. This is a backdoor off-the-fake weave. The baseline backdoor guard X2 should not pressure the pass lane too hard unless a pass is telegraphed toward the receiving position. O1 passes off to O2, moving for a give-and-go. O3 moves into key to receive a post pass, ready to feed O1 and O2 who go deep to the basket, or to fake back and come over the top. Again the defenders should maintain a ballside position contesting the pass lanes and covering the pass lane from the ball as O1 goes deep.

Diagram 5-20. This illustrates double cutters over the high post O3's frontal attack. X1 and X2 should drop quickly to post and roll off with assignments, keeping a ballside position. They should move into the cutter's running lanes and force him wide of the screen, and speed up going over the screen. They should tag the ball as they go by if available.

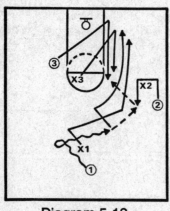
Diagram 5-19

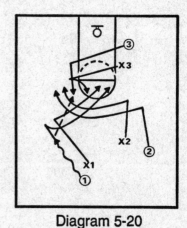
Diagram 5-20

Diagram 5-21. The guard reverse plays backdoor. This results when the defender X2 plays the pass lane too hard. Again this is a question of trying to pressure receiver's possible pass lane, especially if the play is out beyond the key top. The defender coming away from the basket should always be alert for the backdoor move. He fakes up in the pass lane ready to cut back.

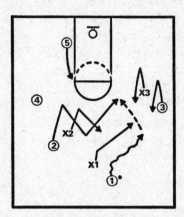

Diagram 5-21

Diagram 5-22. The wing should backdoor when too much pressure is put on the wing pass lane. Quickness should be the answer. Defender X3 should stay between opponent and the ball. If X3 overplays he should release back hard to intercept the pass. Spacing loose on fake down and back makes it easier to maintain a ballside position on the true move to the basket.

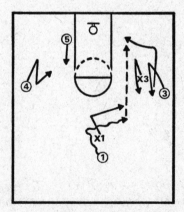

Diagram 5-22

Diagram 5-23. The guard-to-wing give-and-go seems to catch defenders off guard at every level of basketball play. Timing and speed are essential to the offensive success plus the careless defensive positioning and spacing. Offensive wing O2 takes defender away from pass lane, releases to clear for pass, and is ready to double pass back to guard cutter. X1 positions at beginning of pass and should make a quick release back to basket and toward ball in order to force cutter to change direction. Drop-back spacing should cover the fakes and the speed of opponent. X1 should maintain ballside position all the way to basket and be ready for a quick stop and posting by O1. X2 should recognize the give-and-go instantly and play the pass lane with hands and body position. At times he may alter position and move in on passer O2 and force him to move.

Diagram 5-24. Practically all offensive patterns in basketball will have this screen play away from the ball or a similar move from different floor positions. O1 with his dribble draws attention away from the O2 screen moves. Dribbler then passes to playmaker wing O4 who in turn attempts to feed the away cutter coming over the screen, or uses the fake-over and backdoor move.

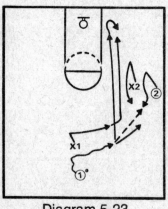

Diagram 5-23

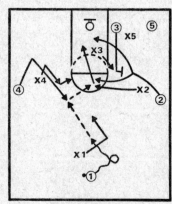

Diagram 5-24

Team defense is absolutely essential to stop this play. The key move will be X2 releasing his assignment, moving in front of screen to eliminate over-the-top phase. He is in ballside position to drop down fast to stop the backdoor move. X3 defender against screen should assume position that does not interfere with X2 moves. X3 should anticipate the screener O3 as he rolls off the pick-for-pass in case defense countered the basic move of O2. X4 has to cover the one-on-one situation. X4 can drop off and pressure pass lanes if assignment is out of shooting percentage range. X4 may jump in to pressure playmaker into moving, thus throwing off the timing of screen play. This move does open up a drive situation by O4. It would be better for X4 to force O4 inside by taking baseline drive away. He has more team defensive help inside.

Diagram 5-25. This diagram shows a complete offensive pattern, with lateral screen executed by wings with O5 coming high to work post passes to the wing cutters. Playmaker guard O1 breaks to right with dribble to draw X3 into O3. O1 reverses to left of key, passing to O5 coming up to high post. O1 continues drive to baseline. O4 fakes down and goes over post O5. O5 may make a quick lateral dribble handing off to cutter O3.

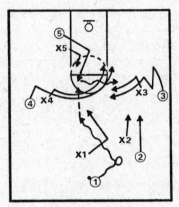

Diagram 5-25

The team defensive pattern should be well coordinated placing full pressure on inside key moves. Guards X1 and X2 should release assignments and drop down to put front pressure on ball and pass lanes. The real key move is X3 dropping off fast toward key as playmaker X1 changes directions. His drop should be to the side of key. This closes possible pass lanes and forces screen to stop in key, costing a turnover. X4 must drop past to front of screen O5, as this would put pressure on pass into post and spoil the timing of play.

X5 must play above O5 putting pressure in his move to post and be ready to keep O5 from getting back to basket. O1 with good timing with O4 can work a moving screen as O4 cuts behind and over post O5.

Diagram 5-26. This diagram illustrates the guard O1 give-and-go with wing O3 followed by O4 over the screen from the weak side. O1 can take any lane that opens up for his move. X1 defending the playmaker should never follow his assignment tight when he moves away from the ball. O1 should never get a ball position on X1. X1 wants to keep stops, slow downs, and reverse pivots in mind as he goes down with O1.

Diagram 5-27. The offense tries to cut your team defense in two parts to divide the attention of team defense. O1 dribbles right, then left, to pick up O4 with a dribble screen executing a single weave at the time O4 is receiving the hand-off. O5 moves out from low post to screen for O3 who comes over the top going down through key, followed by the screen roll-off by O5 cutting toward ball then down through key. X1 should release extra space at the hand-off point to allow teammate to position in pass lanes as O4 comes to the inside. X1 should be ready for O1 cutting to basket if pass gets inside. X3 should release toward ball enough, before screener arrives, so that he has time to go over the top and stop the weakside cutter O3. X5 should play loose on screener O5 to give inside help as well as to go to ball with O5 if he comes. Remember X3 should have ballside position all the way to the basket.

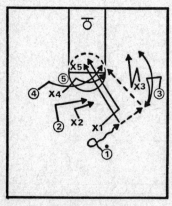

Diagram 5-26

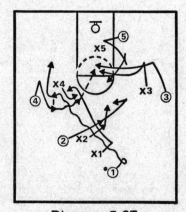

Diagram 5-27

Diagram 5-28. This diagram illustrates a double cutter give-and-go executed on both sides of key with low post O5 coming to high post and getting the pass from playmaking guard O1. X3 is drawn up tight on O3 as O1 fakes pass then hits O5 coming high. O3 keeps coming up until pass starts to O5 then cuts hard. At the time of O1's feed, O4 executes a screen for O2 who comes to basket hard over the outside of screen. X5 plays a big defense if he comes up hard pressuring pass lane. X1 can help by working hard in the pass lane to O5. X2 should stay loose ballside at all times expecting the cut and also expecting stops and turn-ins. X4 should drop deep close to key to help bottle the key. The team defense should be ready as the ball comes across the ten-second line.

Diagram 5-29. Guard to post give-and-go pass. O3 runs a moving screen for O1 then goes over the top of post O5. The offense pattern drops wing O3 to baseline as guard dribbles toward the wing position. Low post O5 comes high ballside to receive pass from O1 ready to pass to cutters O1, O3 and O4 going to basket.

Defender X3 should go to baseline with O3 to cut off baseline cut and force him to come up. He must maintain ballside position and come up over post O5 if O3 continues up. X1 should hold ballside position all the way down through key. X4 should drop off into key ready to pick up O4 if he comes in. X5 should be ready to block any passes coming in, switch as last resort, but be sure to hold position that will block O5 away from basket. X2 should drop in on key to pressure post still responsible to assignment if pass goes out.

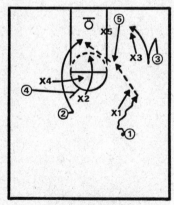

Diagram 5-28

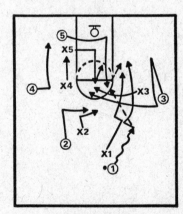

Diagram 5-29

Diagram 5-30. This illustrates O1 guard pass to post O5 with post going to basket after executing a hand-off pass to wing O3. O3 fakes down backdoor then over top of O5 hand-off. O2 moving into safety position for pass. X1 should keep all the pressure possible on playmaking guard O1. O3 takes a screen shot or basket drive. O4 fakes toward post, O5 goes down for rebound. Some coaches like interchanges of O2 and O4 to keep defense away from ball and busy. It is a good move as long as O2 is an equal rebounder to O4.

If pass gets to post O5, X1 should drop fast and keep ballside position on O1 if he cuts down through. X5 should pressure O5 as he comes high and force him toward center of key if possible. If ball gets to O5 hold pressure position until he starts pass to wing O3 then jump to ballside position as he tries to break to basket for return pass. X4 and X2 covering away from ball should drop into key for team pressure and pick up assignment if he tries to cut for basket.

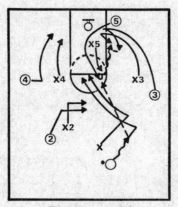

Diagram 5-30

Diagram 5-31. Weak-side post pattern with post O5 and wing O3 work pick-and-roll. O2 and O4 execute a moving screen to free O4 for pass from playmaking guard O1. Two quick passes with three cutters going to basket is hard to stop. Again X1 should put all the pressure possible on playmaker O1. Defenders X4 and X2 should drop inside toward ball. This helps team defense to cover key and basket. X5 and X3 should release instantly toward key as O1 passes to O4. This gives them ballside position and key coverage. They should try to let good ballside spacing eliminate the necessity to switch, which forces a mismatch of forward on center.

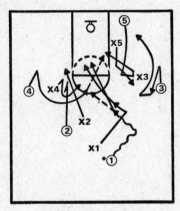

Diagram 5-31

6

Combining Individual Moves with Flexible Team Action

The teaching steps that may be taken before putting the full court five-man flexible defense together are listed below.

DRILLS

Coaches should break the drills down to one-on-one, two-on-two, and three-on-three using guards with forward or wing, and guards with center, or wings with center.

Individuals in all the drills are using their flexible individual moves to counter the opponents' offense with the additional flexing moves that culminate in team pressure action.

The offensive player with the ball will now feel the extra pressure put on by the defender and by the several defenders who successfully cut off the pass lane opportunities. Talk! Talk! Talk! Any surprise movement of a second defender may stymie the dribble move even though the offense may have gained advantage over the defensive man.

Diagram 6-1. This illustrates the basic starting flexible defense drill. The guards two-on-two drill at the perimeter position is basic in establishing the first phase of the flexible team defense. Practice—practice—practice! Guards X1 and X2 should know each other's moves perfectly.

Move by move, O1 and O2 should go through the following drills: O1 sets a dribble screen for O2 to go over to receive hand pass; O1 passes to O2 moves in and sets screen for X2. O1 passes and fakes inside or outside drive, then releases quickly to get pass

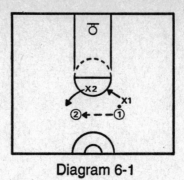

Diagram 6-1

back from O2. Guards X1 and X2 should recognize high screen sets which they can slip, or low screen sets which they can counter by going over the top. Defenders should go to the top of screen from baseline to eighteen feet out. X1 and X2, after releasing to the inside to help against inside moves, must be sure to approach opponent with pressure on outside hand as he receives a pass.

Diagram 6-2. This wing-and-guard drill develops team work between X1 and X3. O1 fakes inside and passes to wing O3. O1 breaks down toward baseline, looking for the pass back from O3 in the give-and-go. X1 should release the instant the ball leaves O1's hands. X1 should release toward ball and basket to eliminate the pass back to the cutter O1.

Diagram 6-3. This wing inside post drill illustrates the team play of X5 and X3. X3 assumes position to shut off baseline drive. As O3 passes into post O5, X3 must release and try to force O3 over top of post. If O3 baseline drives X3 must be between ball and opponent

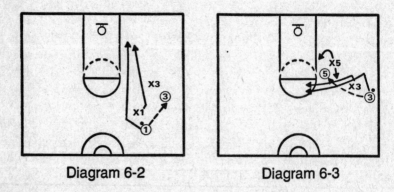

Diagram 6-2   Diagram 6-3

all the way down. X5 must position on O5 to stop his rolling to basket also to pressure pass lane. If O3 dribbles over post O5, X5 should step to fake-switch, then roll with O5. If O5 moves out to pick-and-roll with O3, X5 should step-fake in X3 dribble lane then roll with O5 as he leaves the pick position.

Diagram 6-4. This three-on-three drill working on the outside perimeter with a high post O5 to screen or receive pass from O1 or O2 can develop defensive teamwork with X5, X2, and X1. The drill can be moved to both sides of key as well as the high center key post. You can use three general moves by O1, O2, and O5. O1 and O2 passing to post and driving by on the side where they are stationed or criss-crossing the high post with passer going first or both driving on same side of high post.

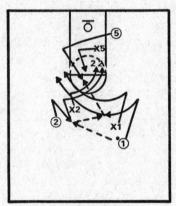

Diagram 6-4

This drill phase uses the guards' scissoring the high post to receive the hand-off. X1 and X2 must add more flexible moves to their two-on-two experience. The criss-cross can be handled by releasing more inches, positioning more to inside, staying man-to-man. Another procedure is the quick drop-back pressuring the post to pick up the cutter comming to your side. Trouble comes to this move when both cutters go to the same side. Defender of second cutter must not get caught up in the post pick. Best move is playing his inside running lane and keeping ballside position to force him wide of post pick.

SYNCHRONIZING FLEXIBLE INDIVIDUAL AND TEAM MOVES
TO BALL AND PLAYER PATTERN MOVES

With inexperienced players, establish a sequence of defensive movements adjusting to ball and man. Take one step at a time. Get the right individual and team movement to drop inside and help to get back on opponent. Each diagram shows new movements being put into the pattern until the five-man offensive motion is complete. You are now using all individual and team defensive skills.

Diagram 6-5. Step one: The four men standing in positions pass the ball around the perimeter, faking passes and change of directions. X5, covering the low post, always in ballside position in passing lanes, ready to break up key with O5.

Diagram 6-6. Step two: Add two new problems for defense to counter. O5 breaks up for pass or screen and O4 executes a cut over post O5—one time with perimeter pass to post and another time feeding O4 directly. X5 should pressure O5 all the way up, positioning to stop any cut for basket if he sees the ball has an opportunity to get to post. The two-on-two drill wing to post will come into the defensive play. X5 should talk-talk-talk so X4 who has pressed O4 pass lane will drop quickly to go over the top of screen set by O5. If post has the ball, defender should drop to a position that will allow him to go down with O4 on either side of post. The drop back may allow him to harass the ball on post for an instant. He should never take his eyes off man completely.

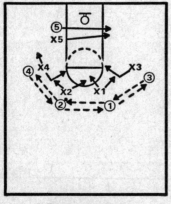

Diagram 6-5

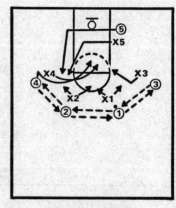

Diagram 6-6

Diagram 6-7. Step three: The perimeter offensive players exchange positions while the post play is going on. Shows the give-and-go move between guard O1 and wing O3. O5 moves away to pull X5. Other perimeter offensive players exchange positions with defenders continuously positioning, dropping back, and picking up.

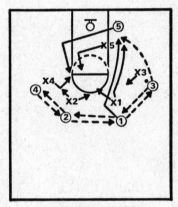

Diagram 6-7

Diagram 6-8. Step four: This is the final drill to develop a complete flexible team defense with ballside and weak-side action. This drill should keep all defensive players moving, talking, positioning ballside on man and ball. With this drill you have developed a well-knit flexible team defense.

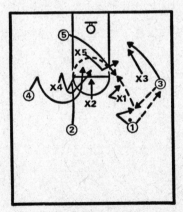

Diagram 6-8

With variations you may fit this team pattern to play successfully against the various offensive plays.

Diagram 6-9. This points up the quick release by X1 as O1 passes and fakes screen, moving through and cutting back toward dribble-driving O2 who passes as O1 gains ballside position as he drives toward basket. X2 should execute two fast ballside moves to stop play. First, drop off toward ball and basket before O1 passes to O2. Second, as O1 dribble-drives right toward key, X1 should execute a fast cross back to ballside position while flying toward basket with O1.

Diagram 6-10. This illustrates the two guards' (X1 and X2) action against offensive ball penetration of O1 and O2. Teammates X3, X4, and X5 keep good ballside position with proper spacing. They drop toward key without losing the pick-up opportunity on opponent if the offensive player attempts to cut back toward the ball.

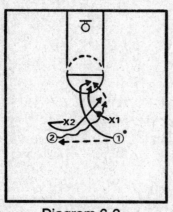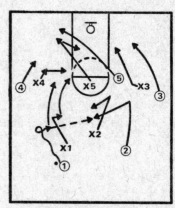

Diagram 6-9   Diagram 6-10

Flexible team defense has several variables to help tighten the key defense and stop individual penetration. You may put one of your best defenders to defend a weaker offensive player which allows the defender to take an overload assignment to press ball and press inside post play to make a defensive nuisance to the whole pattern. Assigning the good defender against a poor shot you would allow him to harass other pass lanes. Assigned against a poor corner shooter would allow defender to drop in on inside posts and lanes.

Defender against inside postmen who cannot shoot outside of free-throw line could stay in to pick off penetration and pressure pass lanes.

A team that over-dribbles allows defenders to mass against the ball.

Diagram 6-11. This diagram illustrates a team offensive move with wings O4 and O3 dropping deep to sideline corners attempting to keep the middle open for cutters driving down the middle. Playmaker O1, driving down the middle, passes into high post O5 who sets to make a vertical drive situation for O1. O1 may drive by O5 with dribble, or pass and take the hand-off from O5, fake to go through, sometimes stopping in front for a shot.

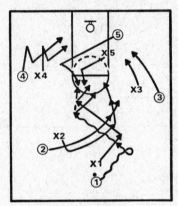

Diagram 6-11

X1 should work hard to hold position and spacing to get O1 to go over high post on his right side if O2 breaks toward right side ahead of O1. This allows flexible defense X4, X3, and X2 to press in toward key with X5 ready to jump the running lane of dribbler. This defensive move can force the penetration toward the sidelines. X4 and X3 defending the deep wings should be quick to anticipate the pass-out in order to get position as the ball hits the wing's hands. Defenders must be sure to cover the baseline drive skill when they go out to press shot.

X1 and X5 should try to bottle up the penetration and not ask for wing defenders X3 or X4 to help. X1 should be sure to flex a quick drop on O5 if O1 executes a pass-in. This puts team pressure on ball and gives X1 time to roll off screen to counter penetration by O1.

Diagram 6-12. This offensive move has a double barreled attack. Left side playmaker O1 and wing O4 give-and-go with a weak-side screen set for wing O3. O2 can move down and set a single screen, or both O2 and O5 can move in for a double screen.

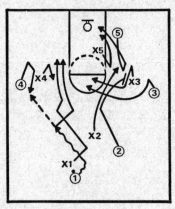

Diagram 6-12

The best move for X1 in countering the give-and-go is the drop-back release toward ballside forcing O1 out of his regular running lane. If O1 cuts behind, keep between O1 and ball all the way to baseline. Be ready for any hook or banana move back at passer O4.

The key to counter weak-side screen is the quick deep release toward key by X3 before the screen can be set. Stay up and drop down if X3 goes backdoor. Leave open only the long court pass.

X4 can add to flex defense by working fast, with position against pass lanes above free throw line extended. Don't put the same pressure on the same way each time. Sometimes drop back 6 to 8 feet and pressure the cutter. X4 can also counter inside O1 screen by releasing back before screen sets, if teammate anticipates and calls the screen. This release would give enough spacing to counter wings baseline and over inside post drive. Other offensive moves may come off this pattern, such as: guard stops screen for wing drive, the start of a weave, and the corner drive pass-and-go. Take away their best scoring move first, then drill against their second-ary moves.

Diagrams 13, 14, 15, and 16 illustrate defensing the three-man weave and its pivot screens. The three-on-three defense moves will be explained in the three-man-weave offense. You can work the front weave in front of the key with a moving double post or verti-cal angle side weave. The front weave gives a greater opportunity for weave to hit posts in a vertical high and medium key position. The side weave uses the baseline and low post position more than the high post. You have individual moves of hand-off roll-in with dribbler; of reversing direction after coming up to hand-off; of fake up and go baseline; of bounce pass to man starting for ball and cutting for basket in give-and-go.

Diagram 6-13. O1 dribbles across ten-second line and passes to wing O2. O2 wing dribbles down and picks up baseline teammate O4 with a hand-off then rolls toward the basket. O4 dribbles up court to break at basket or picks up O3 at top of key with hand-off pass. If O3 reverses, O4 will immediately roll to basket which kills a switch, or may continue dribble weave and pick up O2. O2 will continue the weave and pick up O4, etc. The defender against ball must keep position to eliminate drive at basket. He must release to allow teammate to go through as he guards receiver of hand-off pass. Defender may push out against dribbler if he is going away from basket but ready to release spacing to his teammate.

The defender needs to be careful that he does not telegraph his

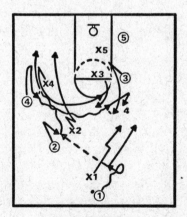

Diagram 6-13

anticipation, and thus free his man to reverse to the basket. He should be sure to lead the ball when going through the hand-off. This eliminates a cut to the basket. The defender of O1 away from the ball should not make an early move to come up through the screen. His opponent O1 can fake one step up and go backdoor for two. X1 should look out for a change of pace in the weave. A quick fake and a hesitation in receiving the hand-off may catch X1 flat-footed if the weave goes over fast a couple of times.

Diagram 6-14. In this variation O2 catches X2 relaxing as O2 dribbles down to pick up the baseline man O4. Just as O4 moves up to come over, O2 slows, fakes a hand-off pass, and continues his drive to the basket. The defense should stay on ballside and concentrate, not anticipate, but be ready for the four moves.

Diagram 6-15. A variation of Diagram 6-14. Baseline O4 starts the same fake up, drives hard for the basket to get the pass from dribbler O2. Defense X4 should be on the ball and not let the first roll weave set him up for a fake-and-go.

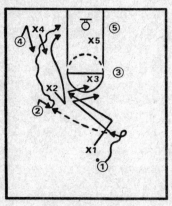

Diagram 6-14

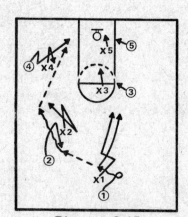

Diagram 6-15

Diagram 6-16. As a variation against defense, O4 should try not to get caught coming up early, but fake back toward hand-off to teammate O2 and look out for a sudden bounce pass. The defense should look out for a sudden bounce pass instead of the dribble with O2 passing to O4, then breaking for the basket, if X2 fails to get a ballside position. O2, instead of dribbling, gives a quick pass to O4 and cuts for the basket on a give-and-go.

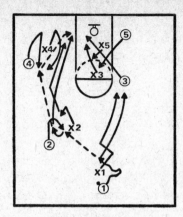

Diagram 6-16

FULL OR THREE-QUARTER COURT TEAM PRESSURE

Your total team effort is aimed at shutting off all offensive moves, especially the inside drives at the basket to force ball toward the sidelines.

Never allow guards or wings to penetrate deep into the key. This puts your defense in the impossible position of either fouling or leaving the underneath man open.

Good percentage shooting relies on getting several inside shots, not outside shooting. Guards and wings should be responsible for containing their opponents, *not* the inside basket-covering defenders.

Correlating individual defense to team defense is the ultimate that you strive for. Flexible man variations should be developed to counter new offensive patterns. Such flexible man-to-man is capable of pressuring any offensive style over the complete court.

Start the team man-to-man defense at the three-quarter court, dropping the defense back quickly past the head of the key after basket is made. With the pass in, the two front line defenders will move in to pressure the ball as advance starts up court. This should be done on time before the dribbler or second pass starts.

The three remaining defenders take forward positions against the opponents and apply pressure to drive the ball to the sidelines. The two closest up-court defenders covering opponents should shut off the short pass from the guards. Make use of the step drilling of two-on-two, three-on-three, four-on-four and then drill five-on-five to develop the flexible man-to-man team knit skill of help in pressing the ball movement up court.

The defender against the ball will try to force it to the sidelines and also force it close to a teammate where a quick two-time can occur. All defenders protect inside and never let dribbler come down the middle of the court.

If opponents choose to bring the third man down to the ball, leaving two men deep, the defense will counter with three-on-three pressure. The back man of the defense defending against their long downcourt men should maintain a front position to pressure coming back toward the ball, but ever alert for the break-away basket cut and for the long pass.

The back defenders should be alert to play a two or three man zone if the ball breaks away from the pressure. Your team defense can be knitted further by all men talking and helping each other.

Diagram 6-17. This offensive 1-2-2 set, from the out-of-bounds, attempts to spread the defenders and put the four offensive men in a position to give them a quick passing lane to the ball. The pattern should spread the defense and still keep the passes to short throws.

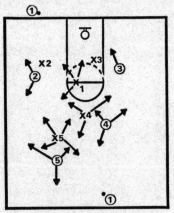

Diagram 6-17

The longer the ball is in the air the better chance the defenders have to intercept a pass.

O2 and O3 have possibly four moves: (a) the criss-cross to take advantage of the moving screen; (b) flaring O2 and O3 with O4 driving middle for the pass, can be used; (c) X1, whose assignment is O1 the out-of-bounds passer, drops back between O2 and O3, with O4 driving middle for the pass; (d) X1, whose assignment is O1 the out-of-bounds passer, drops back between O2 and O3 two-timing their key playmaker. Defenders must take a lead position on opponents in order to pressure the moves and pass lanes. The big IF in their minds makes them alert for the long break-away run to try for a long pass.

If the pass gets in court and passes the defenders, they should instantly release at the start of pass and get back even or ahead of the ball. As the defense pressures the advance of the ball, all defenders should take the responsibility of stopping any dribbler, especially if the penetration is down the middle. Any time the offensive men break toward sidelines, or back toward ball, defenders should go all out playing the pass lane. If defender misses, the offensive player moves fast to get pass. This pressure slows ball coming up court, giving the defender time to recover.

If opponents are slow coming down, defenders move in on the ball and two-time the ball. Against box pattern, the flexing defense lines up with the best defender assuming a position between two close receivers. X1 defender can take off into any pass lane as he reads the moves. He should play ball but watch opponent O1 break from out-of-bounds and play a hard ballside in pickup.

Diagram 6-18. This diagram illustrates the 1-2-1-1 set. The set again tries to force the defense to cover a greater court area and

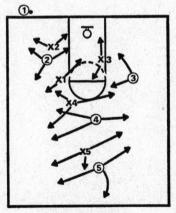

Diagram 6-18

allows them more room to shake off defensive pressures. It does force the defense into more one-on-one play, making it more difficult to two-time the ball and still keep in contact with assignment.

X4 and X5 should be doubly alert to stop the long pass and watch out for a screen. Defenders should play the pass lane, go to sideline hard as offense man must recover and change direction. Defenders X4 and X5 should not take their eyes off the ball as they go up court to defend against the long pass. X1 and X2 can two-time the close offensive pass receiver or X1 can move in on out-of-bounds passer O1 to pressure the pass in. A word of warning for X1 as pass starts in—he had better flash to ballside position on O1 or the driving O1 will get the return pass. X3 covers away from ball ready to cover middle if X4 is pulled away.

Diagram 6-19. The 1-1-2-1 play against a fast press needs the help of screens to clear pass for receivers to get the ball moving up the court. The defense drops X1 back on point man O2. X1 and X4 will two-time screener O4 if he breaks for ball before screening. X3 should be even between the two side players of the triangle ready to break to basket as the second man back. If O3 rolls toward ball, X3 should go with assignment. X2 is a little out of position but should be able to pressure a long pass to O2 if pass is given deep, or to weak side.

If O2 and O3 break toward ball, X2 will have a step disadvantage. X3 may move position toward O3 in order to pressure sudden

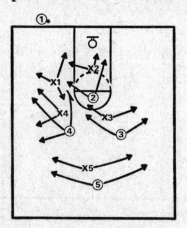

Diagram 6-19

drive to sideline. This diagram indicates that getting the ball on court is a problem. Defense should be aggressive in covering pass lanes and in forcing the offense to come hard for the ball. If pass gets in, all defenders position ballside hard on their assignments.

Your team does not want to gamble unless it is late in the game and it is necessary to do so. The objective is to keep constant pressure on the ball on all close pass lanes and let the offense commit the error.

The pressure should try to break up pattern unity and put pressure on the dribbler to stop and turn him away in his advance. If defenders force opponents to set in other than their basic pattern, the defenders' pressure game has been successful. The professional game magnifies the importance of pressuring on tough pattern teams. It slows down their attack and takes some offense away.

Emphasize again that the defender taking the assignment of covering the man out-of-bounds with the ball should be ready for the give-and-go play. Be sure to have the ballside position breaking with the passer on the pass to the inside.

Be sure to have your defender, who covers the closest pass receiver, fronting and going with his cut. The defender keeps a strong contesting pass lane front position.

Three Quarter Pressure Defenses

In three-fourths court the defense drops off from pressuring out-of-bound passer either by allowing the first pass-in with no pressure, then pressuring the ball and the lanes; or two-timing the pass-in, then going to man-to-man if two-timing fails.

The best pressure man on the team will key the full court, the three-fourths, or the two-timing pressure.

Always protect the inside and vertical court center all the way. Make the ball go down the weakest offensive sideline if possible. If offense gets the ball over the ten-second line, all the defenders should have a good ballside position to force the ball away from the vertical court center. The most important defensive move, after the second pass, is filling the weak side and center away from the ball. Keep the ball down one sideline all the way if possible.

A great deal of the success of the full and three-quarter pressure flexing defense depends upon the confidence the players have in their ability to execute aggressively the pressure at the instant movement of the ball. Having assumed correct spacing positions they also should counter any movement of the opponent by keeping strong ballside position.

A slight indecisiveness on the part of one defender will weaken the pressure if the opponents take advantage of it.

AREA POSITIONS FOR
TEAM AND INDIVIDUAL REACTIONS

Diagram 6-20. This illustrates the changes that take place from full, or three-quarter, press back to a tight key twenty-five foot area.

Area A: Defender spacing against offense to shut off all forward motion toward the ball, and playing ballside at all times. Back two defenders, X4 and X5, are alert for the center-of-court move of O4 or O5 going for the long bombs. Defense has ball position, goes high to intercept or knock it out of bounds.

Area B: Defense wants to be alert and put on extra pressure to slow down the advance of the ball. Remember that regardless of his assignment the close defenders to the dribbler should help to slow him down.

Area C: Defenders away from in-bound position should position on pass lanes but still cover assignment and intercept the long bomb.

Area D: Hard pressure should be applied to slow down the

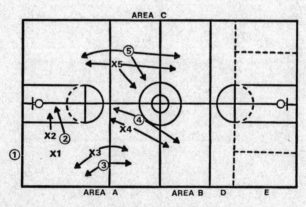

Diagram 6-20

opponent's pattern and keep the pass and the dribble timing off center. Defender should be alert to pressure shots with the area representing forty to sixty percent shooting.

Area E: This is the sixty-to-one-hundred percent area. Defense should tight-hand press, help, jam, and go over the top on the screens.

TEN-SECOND PICKUP FOR TEAM PRESSURE

This team defensive tool can be used against a faster team with success. Defense should pick them up gradually, giving ground but pressuring to slow down the advance. Stop it at the head of the key. Pyramid the team stance to cover the center of the court and to force the ball to the sidelines if at all possible. Make opponents attack on their weakest side.

Diagram 6-21. X1 assumes position on dribbler to give him the weak-side path to take the ball.

He should be sure to have spacing that will handle change of pace, then drive and guide toward the weakest wing. X1 should slow down the dribbler, faking pressure moves as he retreats.

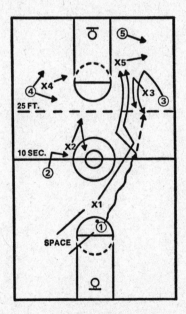

Diagram 6-21

Keep hands working to put on added pressure. Keep position that makes O1 stay on his angle move. Offense may rely on playmaker to bring ball up and over ten-second line with teammates relaxing while moving down. To force dribbler down the side or over to the side as he crosses ten-second line is an important pressure move. Close defense by teammates may add their pressures to force ball to be turned over to the defense. Movements by defense to cut close pass lanes should be quick and force passes down the sideline.

Keep the middle closed.

X2 keeps a ballside position on O2 at all times and should not let O2 beat him going to the basket to get a feed from wing O3. His second assignment is to cut O2 from a pass from O1 that allows a give-and-go.

X3 defending against wing O3 uses moves that should pressure the play pattern. X5 should cover the pass lane from O3 and force playmaker O3 to hold the ball and spoil his timing. X4, away from the ball, should sink deep to the key, aware that a long cross-court pass may be tried to O4. When dribbler O1 starts a pass to O3, defenders X4, X2 and X1 should drop to ball level fast and position against assignments. All this with ballside positions.

Diagram 6-22. This diagram shows an alternate move to force defense to cover two possible moves. O5 becomes the post playmaker when getting a pass from O3. Scoring cutters O2 and O4 come from the weak side hard to the ball and basket off screen O1.

X1 should drop back to the key in the pass lane to pressure the pass to the cutters. X1 should drop deep enough to play the pass lane if O1 breaks to the basket off the screen. X2 should be leading O2 ballside in pass lane as O2 goes down through the key. X3 should drop down in the pass lanes and pressure O5 from the front. He picks up man if he tries to go through. X4 sinks to key as dribbler O1 passes to O3. X4 should be on top of the screen ready to break down to the key in case O4 backdoors.

QUARTER COURT—TWENTY-FIVE FOOT
KEY TEAM DEFENSE

The perimeter defenders generally guard and work as a team with the off-guard releasing to ballside for position to stop dribbler

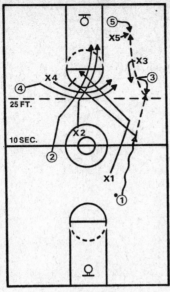

Diagram 6-22

and interfere with the pass into high side post. This defense can be called the twenty-five or quarter court man-to-man pressure. You are now combining individual movements and positions that will pressure individual assignments and positions to harass pass lanes close to the ball.

Diagram 6-23. Offense starting basic post pattern, guard O1 to O3 pass and go through on give-and-go with inside post O5 coming high. X1 should concentrate on pressuring dribbler O1 all the way and slow him down if possible. X1 should be sure to gain ballside position as O1 takes him down through. X5 should pressure O5 who is trying for high post position. X5 should be sure to end up on baseline side, pressuring the pass lane from O3. X3 pressures pass lane from O1 and must be sure to have baseline position when ball hits O3's hands. X4 drops as deep as possible toward key ready to maintain ballside position on O4 if he cuts to basket or ball and to try to force the ball into this collapsed flexible team defense.

Diagram 6-24. Offense finds heavy pass lane pressure on wing O3, changes attack to give-and-go with O3 suddenly reversing into a backdoor play. This helps to relieve pressure on O3. O5 swings across key to open lane for O3, ready to come up and across key if O1 cannot hit cutter O3.

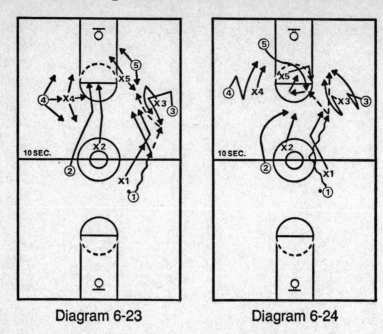

Diagram 6-23   Diagram 6-24

Team defense is similar to above defense with X5 ready to stop O3 with X4 coming down to aid in stopping the penetration. X2 moves down into key area to stop pass that might come high. X1 releases from O1 dropping fast to knit defense as pass leaves O1's hands.

Diagram 6-25. Offense clears O3 for O1 to dribble to wing pass position with O3 suddenly button-hooking at low post to receive the penetrating pass. The second move in the sequence brings O3 across key to screen for O5. X5 should not allow O5 to come across key to receive pass. X1 should be sure to maintain baseline position and pressure pass. X3 should get baseline side position and pressure pass coming in. If O3 crosses key to pick, X3 calls screen to allow X5 to release toward ball, giving him time to slip screen with X3 playing loose in key, ready to come toward the ball with O3. The defender X1 against ball forces it to the weakest side with teammate X2 positioning and moving to help, but keeping contact with his assignment and talking: "Help!" "Clear," "Back off!" "Look out!" "Give," and "Go, Screen," or any other direction that might help. The off-defender X4 on perimeter should also be alert for passes into high post especially with post coming up from weak side. This slow down style of defense is used successfully against teams that use inside screens or against the inside post attack.

Diagram 6-26. This illustrates the offensive fake right-side penetration and reverse to opposite side, forcing the defense to move to new positions.

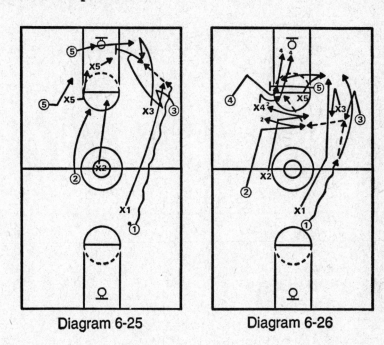

Diagram 6-25   Diagram 6-26

O1 makes his usual penetration drive. O3 suddenly reverses ball to O2, attacking the weak side with a quick pass. O2 passes to O4 going down over O5 screen for a give-and-go. This move is followed by the strong side wing O3 coming over the moving high post O5. This is an example of action away from the ball. Flexible team defense can shut it off if each individual executes his assignments. X1 is always pressuring dribbler O1, keeping angle position, and forcing him to sideline. At the instant dribbler stops and passes to O2, X1 releases deep toward key ready to pressure high post moves and high cutting lanes.

7

Countering with
Individual Floor Situations

Emphasize the importance of keeping ball position against an opponent going away from the ball, because there is a tendency to relax as assignment leaves the danger area. The professional teams have more than emphasized weak-side cutter driving to score off a strong side pass. High school teams seem to be able to pass the ball fast on the perimeter to the weak-side forward, but the defender from his offside position does not get into position as the ball hits the forward's hands. *He should get in position.* Or defender is the victim of a shot up or a basket drive.

ATTACKING AWAY FROM BASKET
WITH FLEXIBLE DEFENSE

Following out from the basket is one of the weaknesses of defense play that must be overcome. If the right habit, when playing against the man going away from the basket, is not developed the defender will find himself fighting through single and double screens.

When opponent takes a defensive player from the wing position down through the key, the player's flexing habits should counter the move by keeping ballside position all the way. *Keep the pass lanes closed to opponent,* until he has gone beyond 16 feet from the basket.

A player must be sure that his running lane is not directly behind his opponent, or any sudden stop or change of direction may force him into a tight body contact situation. If the player makes the mistake of being late going out with opponent, he should take away the easy set shot and force his opponent to move into team pressure. *Cover the baseline drive first when pressuring in.*

With the ball on the outside and the defender's guarding assignment taking him deep under the basket, he should have a mental picture of coming away from the basket fast in a running lane to give him ballside position in the pass lane.

Make a fast rule that every time a defender is taken under and out again, his play must be aggressive ballside. Completely cover the pass lane until he hits the 16 foot mark, when the defender should begin to ease back and look out for the backdoor reverse. Unless the defender is fast, then the defender should hound further out.

Too much half-court playing creates a bad habit and a careless one of delaying under the basket as a player's assignment moves out. One rule must be that *players are always on time and in position as the ball hits the opponent's hands.* Every time a player must go to his opponent after possession of the ball, it will cost points. *Make your opponent come to you all during the game.*

UCLA Capitalized on This Move

Diagram 7-1. Failure to beat the cutter across key at low post is a costly error, equal to failure to stop the baseline drive. The UCLA team capitalized on this error. The careless release by X3 as the

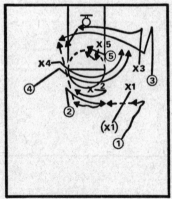

Diagram 7-1

ball starts to reverse allows the screen to work a two-step delay on X3 coming through low post area. X3 releasing properly on reverse of the ball has the same running lane available that O3 would use thus eliminating the screen delay.

O4 rolls across key to ballside over screener O5. O3 drops down as dribbler O1 brings ball into wing post position. O3 fakes up for pass then backdoors behind double screen to take pass from O2 who received a quick reverse pass from O1. X4 must have ballside position coming over screener O5. X5 must release up and into key as ball is reversed. X2 drops toward top of key then into position as ball hits O2's hands. X3 has the tough job of slipping the screens. When O3 fakes up, X3 should follow him from the rear which eliminates O3 beating X3 underneath. X1 will drop in toward post O5 to stop pass to O3 coming up. This is the flexible team play. X2 can position strongly on weak side to make pass tough. O4 acts as second screener against X3 as O4 cuts over screener O5.

The defender can make his vision work 180 degrees by watching his opponent's feet and by moving partial vision back toward the ball as far as possible without visual loss of assignment. Practice the following fundamentals away from the ball.

Diagram 7-2. (Do this from different angles.) While looking over his shoulder for a small vision of the ball and the opponent, player shuffle-steps all the way if possible. He has his hand in the possible

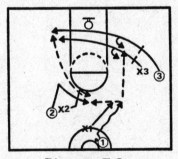

Diagram 7-2

pass lane and does not take his eyes completely off the cutter. The cutter starts from the outside without the ball. X3 should take his flexed facing position. He should know where the ball is and be

sure to have spacing distance that eliminates his opponent's opportunity to turn and beat him to a ball position.

The backdoor move is set up with the playmaker dribbling on an
angle in his usual path, taken when passing to wing O3. O3 fakes
up using the same move he uses to fake the pass at the wing
position. O3 has three moves that he can execute according to the
defensive play of X3. Number one receives a pass going backdoor if
the pass lane is open. Number two button-hooks to low post position if X3 is overplaying to the off-side. Number three is continuing
to the weak side for a weak-side pass from playmaker O2.

Defender X3 should concentrate by the inch and should not
make a position or spacing mistake. X3 should position to pressure
wing pass at all times. Never try to intercept when opposition has
good timing. *When going out, keep back door in mind.* X3 should
keep in mind the low post button-hook move. Position should be
almost directly between O3 and ball. X3 should instill in his defensive countering the axiom: *Never let opposition beat you across the
key.*

Diagram 7-3. This diagram illustrates the fake up over high post
O5. O3 moves to get X3 committed to a front-of-screen position
and breaks down backdoor across key. X3 should drive inside down
to the corner of basket to pick up O3, or move down into pass lane.
O1 angling down toward sideline suddenly reverses ball to guard
O2 who in turn tries to pass down to O3 under the basket. X2 plays
ballside away from O2 and not too low, or O2 can get pass lane
position.

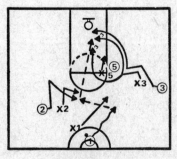

Diagram 7-3

HAND PRESSURE RELATIONSHIPS
IN FLEXIBLE DEFENSE

The defender's hands are very important in keeping the inside pass lanes closed, or in pressuring the ball as it goes through. The hands should be super-active and held in medium position to flash in any direction that could be keyed to a telegraphed pass by the passer.

The hand action against the shot should be well-disciplined to flash up just at the time the ball is in the delivery position to get a clean pressure on the shot without fouling. *Careless hands* that foul at either end of the court and cause errors, especially in the offense backcourt, *are unpardonable.*

Train defenders to fleck at the ball with palms up. There is then less tendency to hit down across the arms, and the balance is not shifted forward by the upswing. The hand discipline should be developed so that the hands never swing wildly at the ball unless the defender forces the ball to be open to his strike.

Defender's hands should be flexible, ready to pressure and attack in all situations. Most of the defense problem areas will have specific hand action to help counter that situation and will be part of the explanation of the problems. The player should remember that he has team hands coming into play, too, as he positions on an opponent. Positioning against the wing with the ball will be baseline oriented and with hand help. Or it will be a released flex if the wing's moves emphasize the inside.

In non-shooting areas against the dribbler, the hands may be down pressuring both dribble lanes with the dribbler moving or still. Pointing the inside hand at the outside hip is always a big help in positioning to pressure the dribble and be in position for the reverse move.

Diagram 7-4. This diagram shows the positioning of the flexing defense jamming the key, ready for board work and ready to pick their assignments if they become cutters. X1 drops down as O1 passes to O3. He should be in position to pressure the pass going into O5 and ready to pressure the return pass to O1. X3 must stop any baseline drive and force the pass. X5 is pressing the pass lane

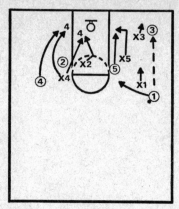

Diagram 7-4

to O5 and blocking O5 from going down to low post. X2 drops to bother O5's movement upward, ready and in position to ballside lead if O2 becomes a cutter. X4 drops to key for aiding the team defense and ready for the high court pass to O4. When X4 goes out, his first move is positioning to stop the baseline drive. X4 has two routes to take depending on O4's move to key.

Diagram 7-5. This diagram shows the flexing defense dropping in on the high post O5. X5 is in up position to pressure pass lane ready to release back and over to stop a right hand dribble drive by O5. This move puts him in a good position if the pass goes to O3. X2 and X4 are dropping in to interfere with the pass lanes and the cutters going to the basket.

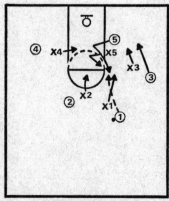

Diagram 7-5

Diagram 7-6. This flexible defense movement should put pressure on O3's dribble and the O5 movement down to low post. X5 should be in ballside position all the way to low post. X3 must pressure and never give up position that stops the baseline drive. X1 and X2 drop down to harass the inside pass lanes but are ready to pick up assignments.

Diagram 7-7. This flexible movement should counter the reversing for the weak side penetration. The team defense should react quickly to the new positions to pressure the offense. X1 should drop to cover inside help for X2 as well as harassing inside passes, also to pick up on opponent O1. X2 should close with position on the left hand dribble and pressure the pass into high post, O5. X4 should pressure O4 going up to 16 feet from basket as well as being ready for the backdoor move. X3 should release lane pressure the instant that O1 reverses ball and release back whether his man moves or not. X5 may front coming across the key but must position behind and ballside as O5 arrives in post position. If ball comes in he should move back to a position that will stop any drives to basket.

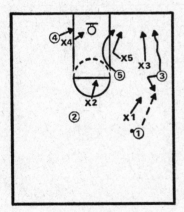

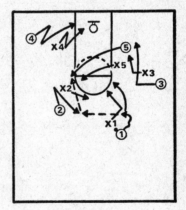

Diagram 7-6   Diagram 7-7

BOXING DEFENSIVE COUNTERS
AGAINST OVERHEAD PASSING

This team defensive tool of boxing the perimeter playmakers can force the offense moves toward the inside. The defender's move can develop into the quick switch, or jump the dribbler's lane with off-side help sinking into the key to trap the ball, or to stop the dribbler and roll back to cover the cutting opponent.

Diagram 7-8. This shows team boxing against playmakers O1's and O2's positions as X1 suddenly moves in on O1. Timing is of utmost importance. X1 jump-releases in from the outside position fast, hands down, then up attempting to force an overhead pass. If O1 has started a pass, X2 releases back quickly to hold a ballside position if he cuts. If X1 boxes in tight he works hard to force a bad pass. He should remember to release back quickly ballside and in cutter's lane. If off-guard's opponent clears out, X2 should yell: "Clear!" X1 adjusts his position to one-on-one situation which is always strong against a right-hand dribble. X2 going from outside box position to inside help should get back on opponent with return pass. *Spacing is all important* because of the overload defense position that the defender has taken. Bottling up a team with good side patterns and excellent corner shots, a player can use this boxing team defense with much success. Individual boxing tools should be applied in specific situations. A player stopping his dribble can be a target of the quick step-in to force the overhead pass. Teach the release to come after opponent's pass starts forcing a lateral direction move by the passer before releasing.

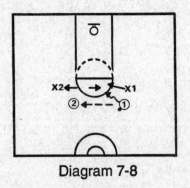

Diagram 7-8

If the defender attempts the box move on a player who still has the dribble left, he must surprise him and force the ball up. *Never let it come down.*

The defender's recovery or release move must have perfect timing in order to handle the next move of his opponent. If his opponent reverse pivots on pressure, the defender's move has had positive results. But he must be sure to release as his opponent pivots. *Part of good defensive play is to limit the vision of the playmaker by forcing him to turn away from the pass lanes.*

Boxing defense is enhanced by using it at the two ten-second line side corners and the two baseline corners. It can be used as the stop of any dribble providing the defender is skilled at getting good position to front dribbler and upon release can handle his opponent.

SPACING AND POSITIONING
AGAINST THE FAKE-AND-DRIBBLE

The fake-and-dribble defense against a quick, agile, faking opponent can be the most difficult problem to solve without team help. Be sure to *teach each defender to develop all the tools at his command to slow down or stop the tough one-on-one player.* You must *build confidence and self-reliance in the defender's ability* or he will begin to use the team help as a crutch. The *defender must build a sense of pride that he can slow down any tough fake-and-dribbler.*

The defender should use all his defensive tools: proper spacing; positioning to drive his opponent away from the key; positioning to stop the baseline drive; constant foot motion; hand lashing in and out; faking-in ready to execute the jump-back release; and never going for fakes, but releasing just a few inches more to be ready for the true move. The defender's failure means penetration inside his team defense which forces his teammate to drop off of his man, hoping to slow the dribbler and to allow the defender to regain position.

Diagram 7-9. The wing position fake-and-dribble is a two-edged sword. If opponent's pattern emphasizes breaking into the key, defender X3 should shift position slightly inside, releasing inches to stop the dribbler. X3 should space correctly in order to maintain position on the drive. If X3 is fooled and loses a little position he should jump back, release for a new pressure position and stop opponent before he reaches the key. The inside foot is advanced to

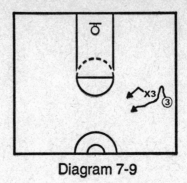

Diagram 7-9

stop the baseline drive without the foot pivoting. This position is weaker to the inside drive. Collapsing defense is a help to stop the key drive. X3 should make use also of the inside foot while going out with the wing to pressure the pass lane, or to steal. By spacing adjustments according to the opponent's quickness, the player has the secret of keeping continuous pressure on the pass lanes of the offensive patterns. Some coaches play the sideline fake-and-dribble with the outside leg up, cutting off the baseline, but this weakens their inside defense of the dribble drive into the key. If this stance fails, the dribbler is free on the baseline unless the inside defense switches out leaving low post open for a pass.

The defender should not allow the passer to fake him into an overshifted position, or diminish his spacing, before he goes on his true move. If defender overshifts to stop penetration, his reverse pivot drive is wide open. He should not forget to use his outside hand pointed at his outside hip as a guide to perfect position. X3 should always use a quick release in order to get back the position. The hard part of this skill is to attack again when positioned.

Diagram 7-10. This shows the dribbler going over the high post pick. The defender should position in the first stage to drive the dribbler to his left. If the dribbler gets his drive started toward the high post pick, the defender X1 should go through over the screen, stay down, arch his hips away from the screen, and take a big step by the screen. If X1 is to be successful in holding a position going over the top of the screen, he should release quickly back and toward the screen, ready to force the dribbler O1 to flair out. This allows X1 room to go over the screen to maintain attack position.

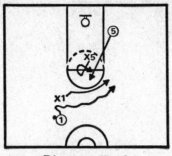

Diagram 7-10

By dropping or releasing quickly, X1 stops the screen shot and the pass to the screener. This leaves the dribbler only the outside shot, which is a better percentage gamble. *Few defensive players make use of a sudden movement into the cutter's running lane before the opponent arrives at the screen.* This would cause the cutter to slow down or flair out, giving the defender room to come over the top.

The jump-switch and the step-out roll-back, or helping by the defender of the screener, should be explained just after the fake-and-dribble defense. These tools give the dribbler an advantage. The defender of the dribbler, losing position as his opponent heads over an inside screen, will call for his flexible teammate to flex and to use a timed jump-out move on the dribbler with a square facing position. The dribbler's defender should drive hard and deep enough to block the screen man from breaking free toward the basket. The dribble defender should redouble his efforts to get into position. This will help to make up for his error. Sometimes the screen, seeing his teammate with the advantage, may move toward the basket before the dribbler defender can get in. The dribbler defender's only move is to dive into the pass lane between the dribbler and the screener who is moving toward the basket. The step-out and roll-back, or helping tool, is used by coaches who do not like the jump-switch mismatches that occur in some switches. The defender of the screener fakes a step-out on ballside to try to slow the dribbler for his teammate, but still maintain a ballside position on his original assignment.

Diagram 7-11. This demonstrates two flexible moves: one, the jump-switch on the dribbler driving on a deep angle over the

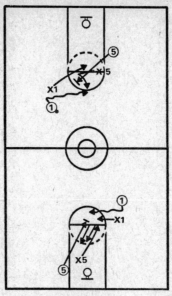

Diagram 7-11

center high post screen; two, the X5 fake switch with roll-back. If X1 loses position on the fake he should drive hard to get position ballside to stop O5 from rolling to the basket. If O5 leaves before he has position, X1 should dive into the pass lane from O1 to rolling O5. This is a last resort to prevent the mismatch of a smaller guard being left on center screen.

FOOT POSITIONING ON FAKE-AND-DRIBBLE

The positioning on the dribbler will flex for every court position. It also should consider the positions of the dribbler's teammates. The side court forward position calls for the defender's outside shoulder to be even with the baseline shoulder of the dribbler. The outside foot of the defender is leading in toward the opponent. This shuts off the baseline drive. The position leaves the defender somewhat weak against an inside drive. Against certain patterns the inside help defense is in position to help. To strengthen the position against a drive, use a half-open facing stance with release spacing to counter either directional move.

The parallel foot position at side court can be useful but needs a few inches more spacing to keep the baseline drive contained.

Parallel feet may be used at the center court against a dribbler who is deadly while driving either to left or to right. If the right foot forward is the fastest moving stance, use it with half-open position which will keep the defender strong on his opponent's right hand but still give the defender quickness going to the dribbler's left.

Put the inside foot forward defending the dribbler on his left side court drive. Against the strong right hand dribbler, the defender must never let his opponent fake him into changing his feet on his in-and-out movement.

Defender should not heel down and play passive defense. He should keep continuous motion in his footwork, and fake in and out. Spacing depends on the dribbler's speed and the distance he is away from the basket. Defender's baseline hand is down, ready for a dribble drive, with the inside hand up in pass lanes and moving at all times to mirror the ball.

The defender should bring the greatest intensity he can command to counter the dribbler's moves inch by inch. Don't allow the dribbler to close spacing that is needed to keep all-out pressure on his fakes and moves.

If the defender keeps the dribbler under control on his first tries to shake defender out of position, the defender's job will become easier unless the defender relaxes.

Remember, against his special techniques, such as change of pace, front cross, reverse pivot, fake reverse, and behind the back dribble, the best counter move for control is to release a few more inches before putting the defense pressure back on again. The spacing release gives more time to counter his true direction.

Step-in fake or rock move: *good defensive ball players are never still but are perpetual motion personified.* With his opponent's step-in fake, the defender should release just the number of inches that his opponent's body and foot move forward.

If the defender releases more than his opponent's fake move, the defender's new position forces him to come forward, at which time the opponent's drive has started. Defender's only other move after this mistake is to try to fake back in with quick little shuffles and anticipate the opponent's drive.

Defender should synchronize his movements to his opponent's

movements forward and back. If his opponent has a good forward, back, or lateral left-right motion in fakes, the defender should release a few inches more in spacing to give him time to pick up the true move. In shooting range the defender should try to find a shot key to read and move in fast, *jumping straight up* to put pressure on the shot. Drill against shoulder weaves, short and long steps backward and forward, fake passing, and change of pace motions. *Don't get caught leaning in any direction.*

8

Countering
In-and-Out Fast Post Moves

The great defensive aims can be summed up in the following statement: *Keep your opponent always on the move and coming to you throughout the game; eliminate his chance to receive the ball as much as possible; use your greatest concentration and intensity to keep him moving away from his special shooting spots by occupying those spots with your body with the goal of cutting down his scoring percentage.*

Defending the low post offensive position presents several problems, especially when there is imbalance between the defender and the post. The smaller defender should always have the ballside position and beat the bigger post to the low position. The defender does give up the board position but the team moves from the top and weak side on the shot, which should help balance this weakness. Using quick front and side movements against the post, the defender may help to regain some board position.

COUNTERING LOW POST POSITION MOVES
WITH FLEXIBLE DEFENSE

If your opponent beats you and gains low post, you should front him enough to pressure the pass coming in. If the ball is in a corner, the front should be from the baseline side to drive him up court. If the ball is above the free throw line extended, line up ballside on the post and cover from the baseline side if a teammate helps on the high side. You should partially face him with one foot in front and arms up in the pass lanes. You should fade with him if he rolls to the basket and never take your vision completely away from him, or his teammates will give him the overhead pass to the basket. Force the natural right-hander to his left-hand dribble.

It is a gamble to position in front of the low post when considering the offensive tools he has. If physically matched, the defender should give him a half-open position on the ballside, which may be the soundest move. He should not play him the same way every time, but move over and around him now and then. And try to keep the low post and the passer guessing on what move the defense will use next, and when.

Remember the defender against the passer should do his job to force the passes to go in on the side that his teammate is covering. He should keep his shuffle moving quickly, sliding his foot and arm in front, and sliding back quickly toward a rear position. He should keep the passer guessing, and keep in mind that the lob pass can come at any time. He should fade with his post looking for a pass but ready to cover the front if the post tries a comeback.

The coach should drill the defender to start with the post coming to low post from different angles. If the offensive player starts from across the key, be sure the defender's position is a little above him, and the spacing sufficient to eliminate any chance of getting beat across the key.

Diagram 8-1. This illustrates taking a complete front position against the low post to force him away from the basket. Keep ballside position. When the post pulls back across the key he may make quick return moves. The three offensive pattern moves illustrate the counter flexible defensive moves. The first, X5 who has

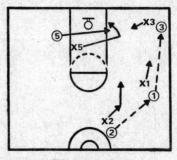

Diagram 8-1

released into the key should stay higher than O5 and lead him across the key to the low post position, with ballside position thus forcing him out. X5 should spread his vision and move to see the ball and O5 at all times. The basic principle of never allowing your opponent to beat you across the key to the ball is the important point in this situation. X5 should be in constant motion to counter all ball and opponent movements. As O5 moves out toward the ball, X5 should move in front to a baseline side position, and baseline hand and foot are in front of O5. Keep the inside foot behind in order to pivot fast to block O5 off the board.

X2 and X1 can drop inside to pressure the inside pass lanes until opponents O2 and O1 become cutters. Never cut the pass lanes completely. Invite the pass and go for it. This gives you a better chance to cover the assignment. X3 can position on the passer O3 to pressure the pass lane going in on O5 right side with X5 covering his left side. X3 should space and position to stop O3 from getting the baseline drive.

Diagram 8-2. This illustrates the second offensive pattern move.

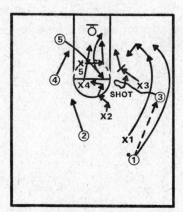

Diagram 8-2

The loss of rebound position by the defender of the low post is crucial. Weakside defender X4 must come in to help. Baseline one-half pivot to front could give him a quick inside position as the shot goes up. This diagram shows the flexible team help on dribbler O3 who comes to the key for a shot. The arrows point the defense movements for going to the board to rebound the missed shot. *Emphasize* the point *that rebounders never get caught standing behind a rebounding opponent.* Play the percentage of getting to any open slot to the basket. X4 covers the weak-side rebound. X3, in pressuring the shot, should concentrate on hand action to pressure the plane of the shot arm action, but not into the arm movement and not pressuring the shooter's vision.

X3 positions to block O3 from following his own shot. X1 should move toward the key as the shot goes up to help on long rebounds and to be in a position to go on the defense at the instant the shot goes up. X2 covers the front and left side of the key, ready for a long rebound and to move out to become an outlet man.

Diagram 8-3. This diagram illustrates the third offensive pattern move, and out-and-in moves of the double post. Post O5 moves up from low to high post as O1 dribbles up toward wing O3. Instead of using the back door and high post feed, O1 suddenly reverses the ball to O2. O4 has gone toward the basket, then comes to high post as fast as the pass goes from O1 to O2. O5 cuts for the basket as the ball gets to O4. O3 cuts off the backdoor move toward O4 as O2 drives outside the O4 post. This attack starts toward the sideline, reverses quickly to the weak side with cutters moving on the passes. O5 pulls X5 up as far as possible. X5 should pressure the pass lane but be ready for a basket cut. He should stay ballside at all times. X3 pressures the pass lane to O3 as O1 dribbles up, ready

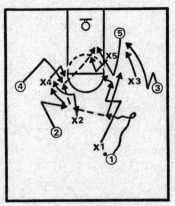

Diagram 8-3

for a backdoor move. He should stay ballside all the way. X2 positions to stop the outside drive and pressures the pass lane to O4. X4 should pressure the pass lane and be ready for a reverse to the basket. X1 drops into the key to stop any inside moves.

Diagram 8-4. This illustrates X1 keeping a ballside position going to low post regardless of what side his opponent passes the screen.

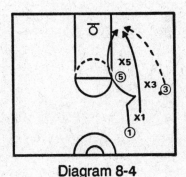

Diagram 8-4

If the post comes down from high to low, the defender X1 should maintain ballside all the way and look for his opponent's come-back pivot to get the defender X1 out of position. He should watch spacing and add release by inches, adjusting every second. He should not let his opponent close it. He should watch out for a step-fake that is intended to fool him into taking the move and opening his lane to the ball. He should force the true move away and be ready for the comeback move. And watch out for O5's drop down screen. X1's added space release will allow him to keep a ballside position.

X5 should not be lulled to sleep when guarding a standing post. X5 should keep his right spacing on ballside and keep the shuffle moving at all times. It is two or three counts easier to start a drive from a moving body over that of a body standing still. The post O5 finds it more difficult to time his break or get a lane to the ball. Call this action: working a defense to confuse the post or the wing cuts. *A moving target is harder to screen.*

The most difficult problem in defending a post play comes as screeners move in to delay the defense reactions and to keep the defensive post positions on the up or out moves ballside at all times. Again be sure that the defender's spacing and positioning give him the time to slide or slip the screen.

There needs to be talk from defender X1, whose assignment is coming into the screen, and X5. Remember a moving target is harder to set a screen against. Hand pressure and ballside position covering the pass lane and the board position make X5's flexing moves a success.

Diagram 8-5. This pattern illustrates the shuffle interchange of wing O3 and post O5 timing with the playmaker O1's movement to gain an open pass lane to the wing position. The offside wing O4 and off guard O2 fake down or interchange to keep defense honest. O5 sets up at low post faking backdoor as screener O3 comes in to pick. O3 should come in on the angle which makes a greater problem to slip the screen. O1, after passing to O5 at the wing, will break away to keep X1 from helping out. The counter play to keep defense honest has O3 breaking to high post with O5 going backdoor.

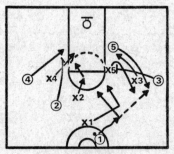

Diagram 8-5

X3 going down with the screener O3 should be alert after the screen and be ready to ballside on O3, at high post. X5 should position above O5 with spacing to allow him to roll off the screen and pressure the O5 pass lane at the wing, ready to go through the pattern again. Offside defense X2 and X4 drop in the key, alert to any cut by their opponents. X3 guarding O3 at the low post should be above O3 with a good release which will counter the drop-down screen.

Diagram 8-6. The drop-down screen by O3 should release the low post O5 to high post or wing. The defender X5 of the low post can slip the screen by releasing up toward the screener O3, releasing up inches toward ballside. He should be ahead of O5 at the screen. By forcing the low post O5 wider over the O3 screen, the defender X5's spacing is very important to stop the up-screen or the backdoor move.

This diagram emphasizes the importance of the ballside position and the release-up spacing by X5 to allow the defender to come over the screen on ballside. This puts pressure on the pass lane and eliminates the O5 screen shot. X5 should force O5 out away from the screen in order to cover O5's break down inside or outside of the screen. X3 should move from the inside to pressure the O3 pass lane with a front position ready to move in any direction.

Diagram 8-7. The defender of the screener O5 should give complete right of way to his teammate who is guarding the cutter to maintain a ballside shoulder lead position. The defender X5 against the screener O5 should realize that his opponent's next move will be to roll for a pass lane or to the basket. This makes the defender X5's ballside defensive position move absolutely essential. Defender X2 should be sure that his drop to the key will keep O2 from coming over him and still be ready for the backdoor move of O2 going behind screener O5. X2 should flash down to a corner of the basket to keep ballside on O2 under the basket.

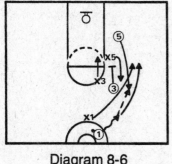

Diagram 8-6

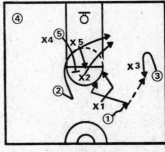

Diagram 8-7

O1 sets up the play with a dribble and pass to O3. O1 cuts away from the ball after the pass to draw X1 away from a two-timing opportunity. O4 drops to the baseline, ready to come to the board.

X4 should release to the key, ready to make a flexible team move in the under-basket passing lane. X1 also drops to the key to stop any moves over the top of screener O5. The key move is made by X2 in flashing back to the head of the screener and ready to stop O2 no matter whether he cuts over or behind. X5 plays an important part of the defense. He should come up with O5 ballside and be ready for a reverse down to the basket. X5 must stay loose from O5 and not get in X2's running lane as he makes the cover moves. O5 may set a post just after the cutter goes through. X5 should be alert for the move.

Diagram 8-8. To get more operating room for the cutters and increase pass lanes, O5 crosses the key to screen for wing O4. O1 makes the entry pass to O3, who moves down the side with the dribble ready to make an inside feed. O1 fakes away ready to come back hard if O3 needs to bring the ball back up. O4 brings X4 above the O5 screen. The best position for defending the cutter is to drop back in front of the screener O5, ballside, ready to counter either move by O4. But X4 should stay ballside all the way and be sure that he maintains his spacing. X5 should position to keep away from his teammate's running lane. He should go ballside on O5 quickly as he moves down or over to the ball.

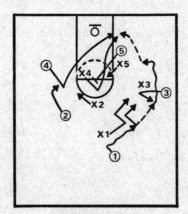

Diagram 8-8

Diagram 8-9. This illustrates a simple screen move that can be very successful. The entry is on the weakside by playmaker O2. He executes a quick give-and-go cut. O2 turns sharply into a sideline post ready to feed cutters O4 and O3 with post O5 following cutter O3. A good general rule for X3 to follow, when defending an opponent going away from the basket up over a high post screen, is to slip the screen to ballside. With O5 setting high post screen, defender X5 should position and space to allow X3 to slip through. X5 should be alert to position ballside on O5 as X3 passes through.

Diagram 8-10. This illustrates a counter move for O4 with O3 faking over the top of screen O5. O4 dribble-drives for the basket, using O2 as a moving screen. O1 moves away from O2 and down. X4 should release after pressuring pass lane. X3 should come through screen ballside. X5 should go ballside enough to give X3 a clear lane to the basket to stop the back door by O3. X1 dropping back on the post should be ready for an O1 cut over or behind the screen.

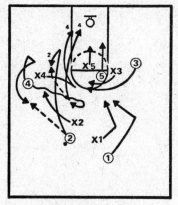

Diagram 8-9

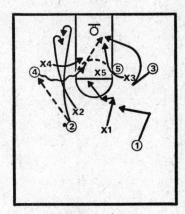

Diagram 8-10

Illustrations 8-11 to 8-13 are simple moves with the ball in various floor positions. The defender against the cutter should keep his ballside position all the way, and come back all the way with ball position if his opponent reverses his cut direction.

Diagram 8-11. This is a simple cut through the key to low post and out to the corner toward the ball. Defender X2 should start with a loose ballside position forcing the cutter to go down to low post and out. X2 never allows O2 to cut over his ballside position.

Diagram 8-12. This illustrates the high post drop down on ballside to low post for a pass lane, then back up to the high post.

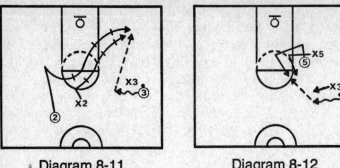

Diagram 8-11   Diagram 8-12

The defender X5 should play the high post with fourteen inches spacing, and play ballside, continuing to play the lane position to the low post. He should play a loose position, cutting the pass lane going down and keeping on top of the post coming up. He should hold a ballside position at high post and be ready to slip back to defense to stop any drive to the basket. He should cover the right hand drive hard.

Diagram 8-13. This is similar to the low post move on O5 with the defender X5 in ballside position going down to the low post with the ball in a corner. A front position, and a pivot to a baseline, makes a half-front position which should enable X5 to get back for some board rebound positions and still pressure the low post up or away. He should keep baseline position closed and be ready to block out. X3 pressuring out on the pass receiver should shut off

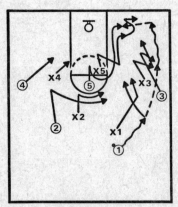

Diagram 8-13

any baseline drive. X1 drops in to help on X3's dribble up out of the corner and is ready to cover opponent O1 if he cuts.

Diagram 8-14. This counters perimeter pressure on the guards. It shows the defenders over-the-top against the dribbler going over the high post. Defender X2 should have a strong position on the right hand dribble. Don't back into the screen. Bring the hips forward and take a long shuffle going by the screen. This helps to hold a pressure position to force the dribbler away from the basket.

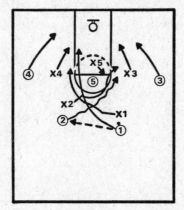

Diagram 8-14

Diagram 8-15. This shows over-the-top defensive move against a single weave by O2 and O4. Defender X4 holds a baseline position

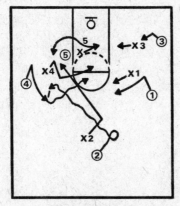

Diagram 8-15

against the left side basket drive, which forces the dribbler to dribble over the high post. Defender X4 should slip hand-off screen and be sure to release quickly toward a position above the screener O5. This allows him to go in either direction.

Diagram 8-16. This illustrates the high post moving out to pick-and-roll off toward the basket. The defender X5 on the post should call the real screen the instant the post takes a first step toward the defender who is guarding the ball on the perimeter. The defender X4 will add inches to his spacing which will give him an opportunity to roll-off in either direction. X5 should be sure to shift to an inside ball position which will enable him to cut off the O5 roll to basket.

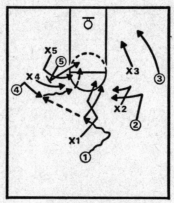

Diagram 8-16

PRESSURING PASSES
INTO HIGH POST POSITIONS

The defender's ballside position against the high post cannot be as exaggerated as the low post because the high post has more operating room in which to lose the defender. *The most common error is to be too tight in positioning and spacing.* The opposition will throw the ball to the post side to draw the defender tight, then return the pass. This catches the defender standing close without spacing to counter his opponent's basket move. The defender of the post, if stationed on ballside, should use his outside foot and hand to pressure the pass lane with twelve to fourteen inch spacing. This gives the defender clearance to go for the telegraphed pass. The spacing is close enough to cover a drop to the basket and a loop pass. *The most important flexing space skill is the ability to make a split-second decision whether the pass will get by your pressure.* This calls for instant release, shifting position between the high post and the basket with the right hand dribble lane absolutely covered. If the high post is away from the ball, this calls for increasing the defender's spacing to eliminate the opponent going lower and across the key for the ball.

Crossing the key: The most difficult high post defensive move to make could be the shifting of the ballside position to the opposite ballside position as the opponent moves from one side of the key to the other to gain position on the defender while the ball is moving.

Diagram 8-17. You must drill this position defense daily to keep the tone. Place two passers out in front of the key with the post moving back and forth to force the defender to move from one side of the ball position to the other. When the post is half way across

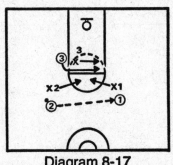

Diagram 8-17

the key, defender X5's position should be behind the post, twelve to fourteen inches in spacing. He should quickly shift to the ballside as he crosses the key. Again, in moving to the right he should make an instant judgment as to when the ball will get by his hand pressure so he can make a jump-back release to stop O3's right hand dribble. X3 gets flexible team help from X1 and X2, who are constantly shifting positions to counter movements of O1 and O2 to put pressure on the high post pass lanes to O3.

Diagram 8-18. Defender X5 cannot guard the incoming pass unless he has position. *Some players are doing a great deal of fouling by contacting the post and trying to tag the ball from the rear.* Defender X5 should not let the high post O5 close the defender's spacing. If opponent O5 can *feel* defender X5, he can beat X5 to the basket with a pivot. Experiment with high post O5 at the free throw line center of the key with the defender X5 eleven inches away, not on the ballside. Have them break down to the low post corner. X5 should beat O5 down as they pass the center of the key. X5 should force O5 to move out of the high post position and keep ballside position if he tries to low post. If O5 beats X5 across the key to the ball, he can go down any time with the pass lane open all the way.

Diagram 8-18

Most of the time the defender can beat the post down. Now set the defender X5 tight against the post O5 and the post will have position to do anything he wants with the defender on his hip. X5 should release toward the ball and above O5's position to force O5 to go down the key with X5 ballside covering the pass lane all the way. X4, X2, and X1 drop toward the key as the pass starts from O1 to O3. X4 drops to the key area ready for a rebound, loop pass, or to beat O4 across the key to the low post.

Diagram 8-19. This drill should be practiced by all the players in order to give them the skills with which to counter ball control tactics. X5 cannot play passive defense just because O5 is out away from the basket. The play away from the basket and the ball offers the greatest opportunities for defensive mistakes. X5 should be in constant movement in order to keep position to pressure the pass

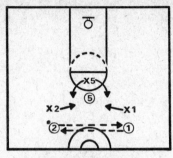

Diagram 8-19

lanes. X5 should cut behind O5 to his opposite side to counter ball changing positions. He should keep ballside if O5 changes position from one side of the key to the other. Setting up the quick move over the top, players may get by from time to time, but they will soon get burned with O5 rolling to the basket. O1 and O2 should pass the ball slowly at first then speed up. X5 should make a quick decision to counter moves if the ball gets by his hand pressure. *Shifting back quickly with spacing release covering the right hand drive,* X5 will have *an important move* to stop the dribble drive to the basket, and should be sure to pressure O5's passing.

X5 should have fourteen to thirty inches spacing against the post at the center of the key. If X1 and X2 are putting pressure on the guards, X5 should have a ballside position, and change as fast as the guards change position of the ball. X5 should be constantly alert for the loop pass as O5 breaks to the basket.

It is a mistake to have X1 and X2 pressuring hard, then let O1 and O2 have an easy pass lane to the center post.

COUNTERING OFFENSE CROSSING KEY
AT LOW, MEDIUM, AND HIGH POST POSITIONS

The defenders should watch out for high posts who like to back a defender down toward the basket to one hundred percent shot areas. The officials should call the foul of contact against either player who moves in. If officials do not protect the defender, his only recourse is to set his knee hard against the opponent's leg to stop him, then release a little to force him out.

The defender should not be fooled when high post moves away

from ballside. He should increase his spacing and keep a position to cover high post on ballside when he comes back high or goes to low post. Hands play an important part in pressuring, but quick shuffle step movement is the only way to keep pressure position. Maintain the ballside pressure.

Position and spacing are the keys to stop good post movement.

Diagram 8-20. Illustrates a drill for X1 to pressure the various O1 moves to the ball. The high post can come towards the ball, crossing the key at any angle. A good post fakes well to get a defender off balance, or plays dead just before he explodes for ball positioning to cut post defender off from the ball. O1 breaks up for a pass from O2. O1 and defender X1 try to practice from each of the six starting spots. Adjust spacing at any position on the baseline that will defeat the post move to gain posession of a pass lane. X1 continues to contest any pass out to 30 feet, after holding a ballside position for 16 to 18 feet.

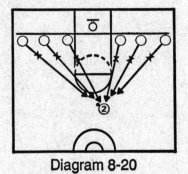

Diagram 8-20

Diagram 8-21. This again *illustrates* the use of the *flexible tool spacing to contest pass lanes and to cut opponent away from the pass lanes. If the ball is in a position to make a vision of both the ball and the man difficult, look at the floor to see opponent's feet moving, but keep a good part of the vision on the ball.* O4 will break across the key first then drop to the baseline and out to the sideline followed by O5 who cuts across the key for a pass and down to the low post. The critical point of defensing these moves by X4 and X5 will come when they position ballside as O4 and O5 cross the center of the key. X4 and X5 should be ballside going down and out all the way. X4 should be above O4 as he goes out toward the sideline. He should be tight while going to open up the backdoor move.

Diagram 8-22. This pictures two cutters going in opposite directions across the key with the ball in position to hit either cutter if they get a position on either defender. Again *flexible spacing and positioning are the answer*. X1 should lead cutter to the center of the key, then stay even until far key edge is passed and ease inside to steal the pass as opponent moves away from the ball. He should hold tight position with no contact. X2 has an easier job of holding a ballside position. This offense pattern has the cutter O1 going first with O3 following, timed, on a pass or a quick dribble move by O2. X1 and X3 should lead their opponents O1 and O3 in order to maintain ballside positions. X2 should not play O2 loose but be positioned to stop any right hand dribble drive.

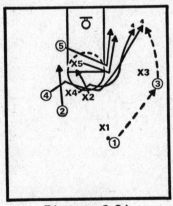

Diagram 8-21

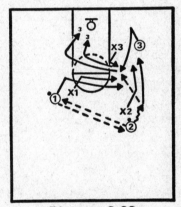

Diagram 8-22

Special Defensive Counters
To Offense Going In-and-Out

The defender will use his space-flexing shuffle to counter the cutters crossing the key at the low post. There is controversy over the position to use to keep ballside position: completely open stance facing the ball, or half-open shuffle and watching the opponent and the ball with the head half-turned. The latter is used here when opponent's moves are blocked, or to eliminate direction changes and to force opponents away from the basket.

Drill your defender to lead his opponent back and forth across the key with his shoulders ahead of opponent as he passes the center of the key. His arm is up on the side of the movement and his head turns toward the ball as he passes the center of the key. Have the post drop down and back up on each side of the key. Have two passers in front of the key to pass the ball between them and then into the under-basket offense man. *Don't forget the rule of pressuring out hard away from the basket for at least sixteen feet before worrying about the backdoor play.*

Don't allow fake moves to lead you astray and give the opposition a good ball position. Here *the rule is to add a little more spacing to give time to counter the opponent's true move.*

Weak Side Drops

Against a tough inside offense the drop-in and swing-to-key away from the ball has a lot of merit. The drills measure the ability of each defender to sink and keep contact with the opponent. There is a great variation in players regarding the distance they can play away from the opponent on the weak side and still counter their opponent's assignment. Some defensive players may drop almost to the key and handle the defense. Others may lose their assignment if they sink more than three rungs.

Diagram 8-23. This illustrates applying the ladder measurement to find how far the player can sink, while watching the ball and keeping his opponent in the proper position to beat him to the ball.

Defender X1 works against O1 positioning according to the ball positions of O1, O2, O3, and O4, O5, O6. If O1 is standing still as the ball moves away to station two and three, X1 is releasing, spacing and positioning to pick up O1 as he moves toward the ball. X1 should maintain ballside position against all movements of O1. X1 should look out for a quick double pass back between one and two, or two and three ball positions. X1 working from each rung of the ladder will show the coach his dropping-off-of-opponent-pick-up ability. Moving the ball to O4, O5, and O6 positions forces X1 to make deeper drops toward key and never allow O1 to come over him thus losing ballside position. X1 should have a strong ballside

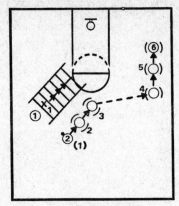

Diagram 8-23

position which forces O1 to go to low post with X1 ballside all the way.

Diagram 8-24. This pictures the vertical ladder at the side of the key away from the ball. X1 and O1 can start from any of the four ladder positions without remaining in the same area. Spacing positioning will be governed by speed comparisons of X1 and O1. Add to this key the ability of X1 to sink toward the key. It depends on his ability to cover O1 ballside regardless of his various moves to get a pass lane to the ball. Add moving of the ball toward O1 or down the key toward the baseline. This will create different cover-

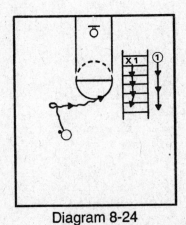

Diagram 8-24

ing problems for X1. The key answer to covering O1 is spacing and positioning to see the ball and the man. The position must be high enough not to let him come over the top of the defender's position which would eliminate his ballside position. Beginners often will start with position then allow a feint by O1 to take away the ballside position.

Diagram 8-25. The defender takes his opponent out and up as far as he can on the ladder and still beat his opponent back to the basket without losing ballside position on his opponent. O1 and defender X1 start at the bottom of the ladder with O1 breaking up and back on the ladder to try to shake X1 from his ballside position. Again spacing of proper inches allows X1 to maintain his ballside position regardless of how O1 breaks. Remember X1 should make continuous adjustments. Again make O1 come to the defender X1 and keep body motion at all times even if O1 stops.

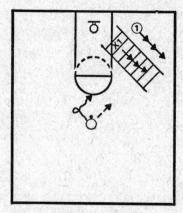

Diagram 8-25

Vertical Screens

Diagram 8-26. Many times the defender can save himself from error by retreating ballside and in his opponent's running lane. The defender X1 should slow him down but be sure not to be the one the officials call on a contact situation. *Stop before contact.* X1 should release back toward the ball and the basket on the pass to O1. Force O1 to change the give-and-go lane, and maintain a ballside to the basket. X1 should be slightly outside of O1 as they get to the low post, otherwise O1 will suddenly stop and fake low post position to receive the ball. Defender should force O1 away from the basket and look over his shoulder for the ball as his opponent goes down key. Defender should look for a loop pass.

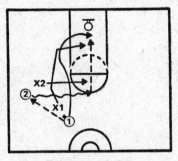

Diagram 8-26

Diagram 8-27. Defender X1 should be ready for O1's fake and dribble drive to the key. O1 may pass to O2 going under the basket. *This drill is especially important* against the vertical screen set by O2 to give the dribbler the opportunity to rub defender off on the screen or force him to release behind the screen and allow the shot to go up in front of the screen. X2 should release or add spacing before the rear screen gets up. Experiment with moving into the dribbler's lane by the second dribble and force him to angle away from the screen. This should be done before the defender allows his opponent to get within eight feet of the screen. The defender has more help inside than outside. His opponent's

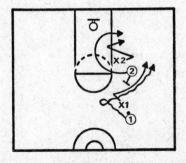

Diagram 8-27

roll-off from the screen is harder to execute inside than on the outside roll. But remember the dribbler may run into the defender as he forces his dribble angle.

X1 should make a quick jump release back toward the O2 screen. He should have enough spacing inches to allow X1 to go over the top without losing position to pressure O1 who is dribbling toward the baseline. O1 will use a pick-up change of pace as he gets to the screen. Teammate X2 can be a big help by calling the screen situation. X2 releases from his screen opponent ballside to help and be ready for the screen roll-off.

SWING THE WEAK-SIDE GATE
TO PRESSURE INSIDE KEY OFFENSE

Every team today is attempting to get greater scoring with moves away from the ball because of the shifted and strong side defense against the ball. The defensive assignment away from the ball now becomes the most difficult to control. Earlier the defender could rest until the ball started around and back to his side, but not any more.

The defensive move of Drop-in, Sink, or Swing-the-Gate, attempts to add pressure in guarding the key until opponent makes a move to become involved by creating new pass lanes.

Some coaches position the player to face the ball somewhat like a zone position, turning the head from time to time to keep track of the opponent's move, then react. Remember a good offensive player is rated on how well he moves away from the ball. My belief is that the defender has the greatest responsibility defending his opponent, with the sink-help secondary.

Consider how the drop-in distance can be measured by using the ladder-rungs-sink or the step-toward-key procedure. First, you must make sure the position of your defender is ballside with spacing sufficient to stop any cutting move to the ball or the basket.

Defensive Cutter:
Running Lane with Ballside Positions

It is important to deal with defensive problems that occur all over the court with an individual defense tool for each situation. A mass defensive drill may give some general mechanics as a starting base in defensive play. But the individual detail for each situation will be the quicker road to success to master the details of the defensive tools.

Once again coaches should recognize the position play which forces the dribbler to create the offensive foul. Many times the officials are giving the offensive man a break in the ensuing contact. This is caused by the failure of the defender to set as he takes away the running or dribble lane of the offensive man.

The defender has perfect frontal position but keeps retreating at the time of contact. Defensive coaches should go to bat for the rule and official recognition that will give the defender a break.

The set should come before contact while the offensive man can make a change of direction. To make our game more balanced, the rule and the officials should grant more rights to the defense. It may take some drilling to get the defensive players to set in front of offensive man to stop his progress or to change his direction. Start with dribbler moving at medium speed for the defender to learn how to protect himself.

A coach cannot have his whole squad execute the sinking-toward-the-key with the same number of rung drops on the ladder if he wants to be successful. One defender may have speed, vision, and ability to anticipate working from a six or a seven rung drop-in. Other defenders may lose their assignment completely with the seven rung drop-in, but they might handle three or four rung drop-ins with less responsibility to play an overload in key defense. The starting five might do it but the sixth, subbing, might open the gates to the offense. Make this tool one of an individual nature by considering the experience and capabilities of each player.

Diagram 8-28. This shows the team reaction to the ball and its movement from O1 to O3 on the strong side. X1 makes the ballside drop as the pass starts to O3. X2 releases toward the key in a position to maintain ballside if O2 moves to the ball and the basket. X3 puts as much pressure as possible on the pass lane to O3. This move forces O3 to hesitate about passing or moving toward the key. X3 should be in position to pressure baseline drive at the time the ball hits O3's hands. X4 moves toward the key to put more pressure on the possibility of the ball penetrating the key. This could be called swinging-the-gate on the weak side. X2 and X3

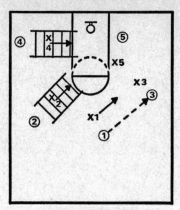

Diagram 8-28

should position to keep their vision on the ball and on their opponent. They should never allow their opponent to close the distance to beat them across the key. Defenders maintain ballside position against cuts from the weak side. Vision is all important; it must be spread to see the ball and the opponent's feet.

The defender should not stand still while waiting for the opponent's cut. He should have constant foot action. This will give him the jump to shut off the pass lane to his opponent. It takes continuous motion to counter every inch that the ball and the opponent moves.

Diagram 8-29. This drill illustrates an introduction to flexible

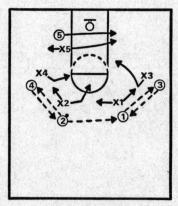

Diagram 8-29

team movements against the ball movement. O1, O2, O3, and O4 pass rapidly around the perimeter. The next phase will put O1 and O3 in motion with O2, O4, and O5 passing. Add the movement of O5 to the high or the low post. Finally allow O2 and O4 to interchange positions as O1 executes a pass to O3. When team defense maintains good positions with weak-side key drops, the offense can add post play high or low.

9

Flexible Man-to-Man
Individual and Team Tools

Adding new moves in spacing and positioning should be accompanied with great desire, concentration, and the will to perfect moves to counter individual and team patterns.

COUNTERING THE OFFENSE
WITH FLEXIBLE REBOUND DEFENSE

Rebound defense can counter twenty to thirty percent of the opponent's offense. This phase of the game is a two-way sword as it controls part of the opposition's offense while enhancing the defensive team's offense.

Some players when going to the basket seem to have a natural skill to follow the flight of the ball and to read the ball's reaction after a shot is missed. Delay and timing is done away from the basket. They move in with short quick steps until the jump-timing triggers their drive to go up on any step as they read the ball off the board.

You should be very exacting in teaching rebound mechanics in every drill used to get maximum results. The rebounder should never let the ball come to him. If he makes a mistake it should be made when he is in the air—he should never be caught standing.

The rebounder's effort must be high and hard. He should go up into the ball with wrists close together, fingers cupped, ready for the pressure thrust into the ball while attempting to extend up and forward with a twisting motion for eliminating other hand pressures that may be coming in. He should bring the ball into his

shoulders with elbow protection turned to get his right hand back
of the ball, cocked ready to throw before he hits the floor or after
landing. His head is turned on the way down as he looks for his
prime outlet pass receivers. He is also observing the opposition
lane pressures. This is all a basic part of his throwing judgment.

Most rebounder's mistakes are made in timing the move to the
basket. Many rebounders are caught standing upright and must
coil before going up. This allows a quick, smaller man to beat them
to the ball.

Some rebounders are caught coming in too early and are standing as the ball hits. Unless your player is a super leaper, this
position is weak. A moving rebounder gets extra power in his leap
and has body pressure advantage in the board fight.

Rebound Drills and Skills

If the defender is taken under the basket as a shot goes up, teach
him to take two or three small steps out then back in for the
rebound. I firmly believe the rebound skill can be taught to all
players regardless of their size. *But they need practice and much
experience.*

Fear holds back some players just as it does when they put on
boxing gloves for the first time. Actually if you prepare a little
contact practice for the rebounder to give him confidence to go
hard at it, the battle to teach good rebounding is more than half
won. Be sure to tape players' ankles well. Tell them to be physically ready for contact.

Never let your players get caught standing behind or moving in
back of an opponent who has managed to get position coming in to
rebound. Play the percentage rebound and go for any open slot.

Be sure your players start rebound movements from different
floor positions. In our case, our success in out-rebounding the
opposition was due to moving and to changing the practice situations in rebound development.

Diagram 9-1. This diagram illustrates rebounding starting points
from seven floor stations. Rebounding practice starts at the top of
the key with the stations approximately the same distance from the
basket. Rebounder X1 learns to judge how much time can be taken
to practice his blocking off the shooter from the basket, go hard and
high for rebound.

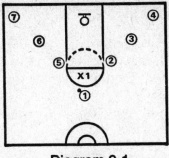

Diagram 9-1

Start the blocking picks with this drill, or add it to the 9-2 drill. It is essential to use vertical vision and rotation of the head to move upward toward the flight of the ball without losing complete vision of the offensive rebounder. This is very important in developing efficient rebound skills. Actually spread the vision with upper half picking up the flight of the ball and the lower part picking up offensive rebounder's running lane. At the same time see the open lanes to the basket to allow a drive through without fouling.

Diagram 9-2. The three-man rebound drill: O1 dribbles down to give O3 a screen which adds to the blocking-out problems. X1 should move down with O1 and give enough space to allow X3 to work against O3's shot and his drive to rebound the ball. X3 should come over the top of O1 and beat O3 up to the hand-off. If the position is lost, X3 pressures out on the right hand, calls the shot and is ready to read his first move to the basket. X3 blocks out, releases, and goes to the ball. X1 should not be tight to the dribbler to allow X3 space for movement. X1 blocks and takes inside re-

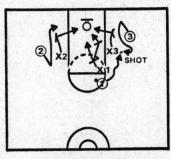

Diagram 9-2

bound lane. X3 blocks and takes outside lane. Rebounders should time their release and go to the board high for a rebound. The closer X3 blocks out to the board the quicker he will release and get into the board. *The biggest error in rebounding is to get in too soon and go too far under.* A non-pressure shot when missed will be short. Pressured and hurried, if missed, the shot will be long. Be sure the defense has the side away from the shot covered.

Diagram 9-3. Move this drill to each sideline for floor position changes. This varying of floor positions gives greater experiences in making and timing the moves. *Drilling from only two or three spots does not do the teaching job.* Varying of floor positions will bring about flexing the checkout times according to position and distance the shot is from the basket. It also brings about more experimenting in flexing position changes to give the advantage needed. O2 dribbles and passes to O1 for shot. X1 and X2 yell "Shot!" and go to the board.

In our case the three-on-three check-out called for the ball to reach the floor after the shot while practicing to compensate for the height advantage of our opponents. This exaggerates the holding blockout position before going for the ball.

Diagram 9-4. X3 may shoot at any time along the dribble. The three-on-three, as in other diagrams, does not show the flexing details absolutely essential to success. Each shot position and distance away from the basket demands some flexing of position on the part of the defender. Don't be mechanical with only one rebound tool. For example, the short shot does not give time to position, check, and go that the outside shot gives. Angle floor

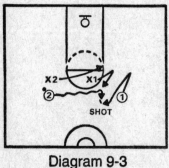

Diagram 9-3

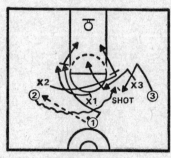

Diagram 9-4

position check-out calls for specific details in check-out and re-bounding. Shot position taken on an angle line from the basket seems more difficult to keep off the board.

O1 clears middle allowing O2 to dribble over the key and pivot pass to O3 for the shot. X2 should hold position but release to allow X3 to come through. On X1, X2, and X3 block and go to the board.

Diagram 9-5. This diagram shows the pivot shot off the dribble when the defensive man X3 positions too much on the outside ball position. I believe every offensive player should have a pivot shot. It is the most difficult shot to guard. X3's position should be with his left hand pointing at the shooter's inside hip. His guarding movement must be under control in order for X3 to get pressure up on the shooter's right hand. X3 should not let the dribbler fake him to overplay when dribbling left. X3 should never let O3 back into the key with a reverse dribble. X3 should go straight up to pressure the shot.

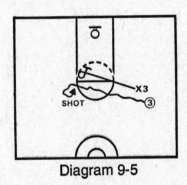

Diagram 9-5

Diagram 9-6. This drill is needed to teach rebounders how to slide by rebounders under the basket without fouling. O4 and O5 are just standing under the basket to give X1 and X3 an opportunity to find open rebound slots. This gives practice in positioning against opponents with the check-out move. The rebounder should follow the shot, and go up high and hard for the rebound. Point out the importance of covering the weak-side slot by the rebounder closest to the basket. The pressured shot is often missed by over-shooting. The non-pressured shot is often short when missed.

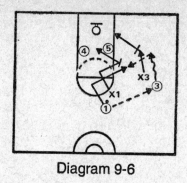

Diagram 9-6

Diagram 9-7. This illustrates a rather negative approach drill for rebounding which finds X4 caught out of position back of O4. Some players develop the habit of quitting on the rebound from this position. Practice can instill the habit of never standing behind an opponent. Defenders should drive for any open slot playing the percentage. X1 can practice pressuring shot hand, check out, and go for rebound. Teach the right or left leg take-off driving up and in the direction of the ball path off the board or iron. Such flexing can be designated as going for percentage rebound position. Teach the body pivoting against pressure as it leaves the floor. Another good rebound skill is moving in to rebound, pushing off toward the side line when leaving the floor. This move clears for a pass out.

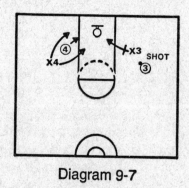

Diagram 9-7

Be sure to point out the differences between just rebounding and detailed rebounding. The check-out and moving in may be the same, but the hand action and thrust into the ball with pressure on the upward and forward twist on the ball, are some of the details for superior rebounding.

Even some experienced players have balls knocked out of their hands after possession. But the only time the rebounder should lose the ball he has rebounded is if opponent tries to throw him and the ball through the hoop. In other words *never release the ball, but gain control to pass to outlet men.* The superior rebounder has developed superior vision, picking up the flight of the ball by the time it reaches the apex of the arc, still seeing his opponent's movement with vertical (not horizontal) vision. Without any loss in reading the ball's flight and hit, this vertical vision picks up the rebounder's position and the open slots to move through without fouling.

Players should look out for the offenses' double whammy: pressuring the defensive rebounder with grabbing hands and with ball pressure on each side of rebounder. The rebounder should try not to pass off at top of his rebound if under pressure but pull the ball hard down to the floor. He should swing one of his legs back with the ball as he reverse pivots and cuts out.

Rebounders should develop several deliveries that accurately and quickly get the ball to the outlet man. Side arm, underhand, hook, bounce, baseball, and chest passes should give him lane opportunities to deliver the pass. He should develop fakes that will cause the defender of the pass to commit himself, then execute the pass that will reach the outlet. Defending the rebound is not completed until the ball is passed safely into the hands of a teammate.

SLIPPING THE SCREENS WITH FLEXIBLE MOVES

Several details of flexible team positioning of defenders should be so disciplined, developed and over-learned that the pressure of exchange in offensive players' positions will not cause loss of good moving counter positions. It is a part of the total team defensive flex in positioning while the ball is in constant motion, as well as the opponents' changing positions.

A good place to start learning and drilling specific space and position movement should occur out in front of the key area. Put two defenders against two offensive players whose motion will be lateral across the floor, using the pass and dribble exchange in moving the ball. The offense expects to slow down one of the defenders and thus gain a position to further penetrate the defense. A defender working against the ball must have the right-of-way always. Spacing of each defender on his opponent should be the same throughout the action with constant flex adjustments. Remember the defender against the ball is always inclined to be sucked up toward the ball, thus creating the desired move for the offense to gain the advantage.

During this action a side screen may come in on the defender who will make a quick sliding move back of the screen but still ahead of his opponent. The defender should stay low and increase his shuffle-foot speed as he slips back of the screen leading the offensive opponent, and thus eliminating the opponent's chance to drive for the basket. Come through ahead using a long glide step through screen position. This gives a chance to pressure the shot if opponent stops in front of the screen.

Warn the defender not to move behind both the screener and his teammate. Such a move, if it becomes a habit when executed within shot distance of the basket, will give the defender's opponent the non-pressure shot. The defender will find other moving screens coming between him and his assignment. Also, his opponent's passing can be executed without any pressure on the pass lane.

Diagram 9-8. This illustrates the sideline *slipping the screen* action with the ball moving away from the basket. X4 defending against dribbler O4 has shoulder play loose which allows X1 a pass through hand-off. X1 giving room and position to counter hand-off receiver O1, X1 should hold position and be ready to move through the screen fast. O1 might go through, then stop and reverse back over the dribbler.

Diagram 9-9. This illustrates the *over-the-top* move against the double key screen. X4 on the strong side should drop to the front of top screener O2. This eliminates the key move on this pattern. Ball is moved toward wing and passed to O3 by O1 who breaks back away to keep O3's inside pass lane open. If O4 fakes over and goes down backdoor, X4 should drive down to the corner of the basket to counter the move. X5 guarding low screener O5 should keep X4's running lane clear but be ready for O5 flashing across to the

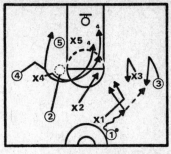

Diagram 9-8	Diagram 9-9

post and receiving the pass from O3. X2 drops into key ready to stop inside the pass and the ballside position to pick up O2 if he cuts.

Diagram 9-10. This diagram illustrates a *hand-off weave* at the head of the key. X2 covering dribbler should have absolute position with O2 angling toward the basket. X1 maintains ballside position on O1, with O1 going away and over the dribbler. X1 can put extra pressure on O2, the dribbler, by jumping his lane. X1 should be aware of O1 turning down the key after passing the screener.

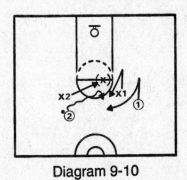

Diagram 9-10

DOUBLE SCREEN PATTERNS

Diagram 9-11. This illustrates the flexible team defense to counter the strong-side cutters coming over the double screen away from the ball. It shows the importance of spacing and the position of each defender to help keep lanes open for teammates to maintain ballside position and to cover the pass lanes to their own

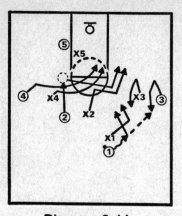

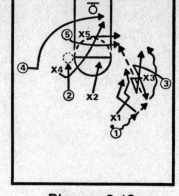

Diagram 9-11   Diagram 9-12

assignments. As the ball is moved to pass lane positions by O1 and O3, the strong side is setting up the strong-side double screen. O5 and O2 double screen. O4 is moving to take the defender X4 out of good defense position. He cuts over double screen in time with O3 passing. The key move of X4 is to release from O4 dropping to top of the double screen. From this position X4 eliminates the over-the-top double screen pick, besides having a straight lane to the ballside low post fronting O4 if he moves to low side behind double screen. Leave open just the long looping pass.

X5 defending O5 should stay close until X4 goes down through, then quickly release space toward the ball. X2 follows O2 down to set the up side of the double. X2 should space loose toward the ball which allows X4 to drive down the key unmolested.

Diagram 9-12. This illustrates O4 faking over the top of double screen, then cutting backdoor below the double screen. X4's flexible tool to counter backdoor is the same as used to stop over-the-top move. Teammates take and hold the same positions, as X4 drives down the key to intercept O4 coming under. X5 should give teammate X4 a clear lane to corner of the basket. X5 wants to be alert as O5 flashes to the post just as X4 goes by.

Diagram 9-13. This illustrates the double post screen action with O4 dropping deep behind the screens to a position to allow him to go backdoor, or up over the top of the double screen. X4 should position to stop the backdoor with X5 playing loose toward the ball to help. X4 tries to force O4 up, going over the top. X2 releases

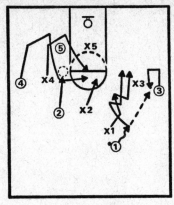

Diagram 9-13

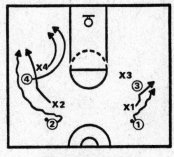

Diagram 9-14

toward the ball to slow down the pass to O4 to give X4 time to recover his lost position.

Diagram 9-14. Flexible team defense must constantly adjust the countering action according to each spot on the floor. Position of the offensive action should decide all flexible action for countering successfully. The diagram at the left side of key illustrates X2 slipping the screen going down the sideline with O2 the dribbler. The key move by X2 is to have shoulders ahead of O2 as they pass the screen O4. X2 should be alert for a change of pace at this time. X4 should release and position to give X2 all the running lanes he needs to control dribbler O2. Illustrated on the right side of the key is an over-the-top by defender X1. If O1 dribbles in a vertical direction down at screener O3, X1 should release for more spacing before he gets to the screen. With extra inches X2 may pressure the dribbler and force him wide, which gives him a chance to go over the top successfully. X3 should talk to X2 to give him position on the screener O3. X3 releases inches to keep out of X1's running lanes and be ready to stop the play.

Not to release before the screen hits is a defensive weakness. The defender should make a quick move into the dribbler O1's lane to force him to go wide of the screen. The defender should quicken the pace to pass the screen, ready to release back if the position is weak, and attack again after gaining position.

Diagram 9-15. Left side play has dribbler O4 going over screener O5 at medium or low post. X4 should first position to stop

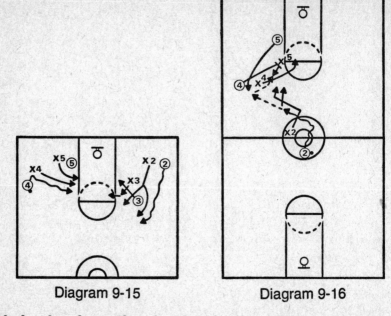

Diagram 9-15   Diagram 9-16

the baseline drive. Then, knowing that the screener O5 is setting at key, X4 should space enough inches to give him position to force the dribbler up enough to be able to go over the top in position. Right side play dribbler O2 fakes the baseline, then drives up over high post screener O3. X2 must make a decision whether to position to push the dribbler out and go over the top of screen or slip by going inside. If this move is in high shooting percentage area, he should go over the top. X3 should stay loose with spacing to let X2 have the lane and be ready to help if X2 gets into trouble.

Diagram 9-16. This is the key move of the *shuffle motion* offense. This diagram illustrates the wing screening down to release O5. It is used especially against tight pressure defense to make pass to O4 difficult. One key for X5 to use in forcing the screen to leak will be the positioning against the incoming screen. If it is high coming in, slip the screen. If it is low, go over the top. X4 guarding O4 should not interfere with X5 but still drop deep enough to stop any loop pass to the basket. X2 should release back toward the key, ready to help and still pick up the breaking assignment. X5 should be in continuous motion, and release up away from O5 before the screen gets in.

FLEXIBLE TWO-ON-ONE TRAP MOVES

A number of positions on the floor lend themselves to a quick two-timing trap move such as two-on-one with the dribbler moving over the screener, or the pass moving into a receiver with the passer breaking over the receiver.

Whenever the move has the driving threat moving away from the basket, the defense should be alert to take advantage and tie the ball up or execute a steal.

All three diagrams illustrate situations where the ball starts from the outside perimeter going down the side and coming back out, which give ideal opportunities for two-timing the ball.

The first move is possibly the most extreme of all our flex skills that make us pay a high price for failure. It may not be sound practice to have your whole squad get the green light for its execution. Two or three squad members who work the outside perimeter defense assignments may have the quickness, experience, and judgment to be successful in executing the two-time trap flexible defense move.

As with every other difficult skill you must *practice and practice* your squad in the execution of the two-time defense. It then becomes an efficient defensive tool to stall part of the offense's pattern. It is also a necessary tool to work efficiently against the ball control patterns.

Remember the move is made to two-time after the ball passes the screen which gives possibly a three-count opportunity to come in on the opponent's blind side while a defensive teammate gives the dribbler maximum pressure. Confine trapping to specific floor areas to be used in special situations. Practice and practice to keep it toned, or lose points.

Diagram 9-17. This illustrates a two-timing of the dribbler going down toward the baseline over the screener O4. If dribbler O2 has an even or ahead position, X4 should slip the screen and speed up in order to stop O2 from turning toward the basket. Just as soon as the dribbler loses vision of X4 going down, X2 will flash up on the outside of O2 as X4 pressures O2 to stop or change direction. X4 will flash in front of O4 as he receives the hand-off. X4 and X2 should time together, or O2 will roll to the basket free.

Diagram 9-18. This illustrates the dribbler O1 breaking toward

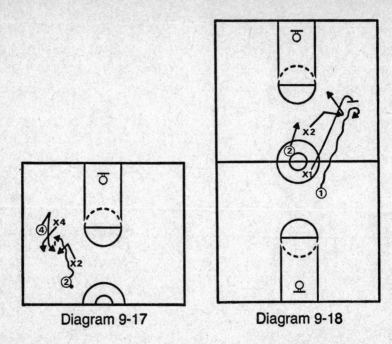

Diagram 9-17   Diagram 9-18

the sideline as he brings the ball over the ten-second line. X1 should have a good front position to stop the dribbler or to force a change of direction. The key to success is X2 timing his move from a position close enough for X2 to leave his assignment and put pressure on at the stop or turn of O1. Be sure to drill each player regarding the distance he can travel to double-team successfully.

Diagram 9-19. When offense brings a second player near the ball, away from the basket, the two-time potential is great. This play needs the help of surprise to assist in its success. O5, the high post, is dropping down to screen X4 who is defensing the dribbler O4. X4 should have good position coming over the top of the O5 screen. X5, coming down with screener O5, should make the quick-jump dribbler's lane move. This is a dangerous flex move that must be timed, tying up O4 before he can pass. Flex team positions are shown, to help out if trap fails.

FLEXIBLE COUNTER MOVES AGAINST BASELINE PLAYS

Flexible positioning enhances success in countering the strong baseline drive offensive weapon. Practice this counter move con-

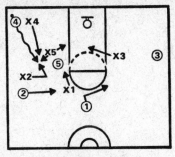

Diagram 9-19

tinuously in order to solve the defensive trouble found at high school, college, and professional levels. Too much fouling and scoring takes place in this situation.

The shuffle-step foot position against the baseline drive has three countering moves now being used by many coaches. The first is: if the dribbler's position is close to the baseline, the baseline-side foot of the shuffle is forward, forming a boxing position to force the dribbler away from the baseline and up. The second is: the baseline foot back allows the defender to start his instant shuffle retreat move without executing a foot pivot exchange. The third is: moving in tight with parallel feet which makes the move similar to boxing the corner. Fake the dribbler with both arms down.

I tried the first and third baseline positions with fair success. Some smart offensive players receive passes 5 or 6 feet away from the baseline, then proceed to drive against the baseline forward foot—and too often get the drive by. If this foot position is flexed too far toward the baseline, it develops an over-compensating flex. The baseline foot forward position does not do the job as well as the baseline foot back. It has release motion before the pivot.

More team help is available up and inside the key compared to help on a baseline mistake. Also many players become deadly shots just after they defeat the pressure. I prefer to let the fake-and-dribble go against the forward foot away from the baseline. It handles more situations. Remember your only good counter space releasing move against a dribbler, who tries to fake you up court away from your good baseline position, is a shuffle quick-step back to increase spacing distance 6 to 8 inches. This gives an extra count to counter offense's true move without loss of position or changing of feet. Warn players to be alert for opponent's step-fake and pull-back into shot position. If they over-compensate with release against the fake, the drive will get by. The shot pressure hand should be ready at all times and the dribble hand pressure should be ready for the drive.

If the defender is in the correct position to stop the baseline drive, it gives him extra time to maintain position when the opponent comes over the top of his lead foot. Make a quick jump-back and pivot to press up as opponent goes toward the key. Don't forget the constant body motion working in quick short faking body motions in-and-out without commiting oneself. Remember, if the dribbler steps into the defender, the defender should flex just enough spacing so that a forward break step cannot get the opponent the position he wants. If defender over-releases, the opponent's shot goes up or defender rushes back in and allows the dribbler to go around.

If defender ever over-shifts on opponent's fake away from the baseline, he will turn opponent loose on the baseline. The best move against the good fake is a 6 or 8 inch flex back. Once the defender starts opponent up on the angle toward the head of the key, the defender must never let him off but be alert for a reverse. Again the exacting, disciplined flex position is very important to counter this tough move.

Nine times out of ten if the reverse dribble pivot is losing your defender, he is over-compensating in the moving direction and is being sucked in too tight, which is a guaranteed sign for the dribbler to reverse drive.

FLEXIBLE COUNTER TO INSIDE KEY DRIVE

The most popular basic set pattern used at all levels today is the two-way attack against the defense. First, the guard playmaker exchanges position at court side with the wing who hands the ball back to the guard executing an inside screen or moving to guard position. Second, this move forces the defender to defend the baseline drive and the inside drive over single and double screens with pass-offs if the defense shifts. The drive into the middle seems to be two edged. One, it flattens out the defense, allowing close-in outside shots to go up without pressure. Two, it makes things

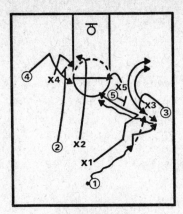

Diagram 9-20

happen to inside defense, such as giving up a close inside shot and allowing the offensive rebound to have inside positions for the missed shot.

Diagram 9-20. In this diagram the offense is attempting to keep the flexible team busy with individual assignments along with a continuous ball movement. Always ask defenders to keep their mind's eye on the ball regardless of offensive gyrations. O1 moves the ball to wing O3 who in turn passes back to O1 and rolls down toward the basket, then hooks back to a posting position. At the same time the inside post O5 will move out to screen defender X1 as O1 drives over screen O5 to the basket. O5 after screening rolls toward basket with O3 coming in behind for a pass or rebound. O2 and O4 interchange away from ball hoping to keep X2 and X4 honest and ready to take a feed from the strong side.

The flexible defense should be ready to close on any cutter besides making quick recovery on individual assignments. X1 should play O1 loose on this play in order to pressure O1 going in either direction. Also go over the top of screener O5 to stop O1 from deep penetration. X3 will keep ballside position going away from the ball and be ready to pressure the pass lane when O3 button-hooks. X5 will call screen, and play loose on the screener O5 in order to help stop the penetration. He also can execute one dangerous flex move, that of following screener O5. He can step out into dribbler's lane two counts then roll back ballside with O5 if he rolls to the basket looking for the loop or bounce pass. X5 puts momentary

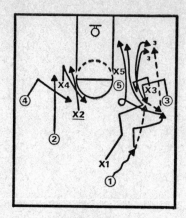

Diagram 9-21

stop on O1's dribble drive. X1 should recover from the screen delay.

Diagram 9-21. This diagram illustrates the secondary move off of play 9-20. X3 should pressure pass from O1 to posting O3. X5 will move ballside of O5 to stop the pass if O5 moves in. X1 will release toward the ball and then follow assignment.

FLEXIBLE TEAM-DROP DEFENSIVE COUNTERS TO OFFENSIVE PENETRATIONS

Flexible man-to-man defense should have team movements to counter any breakdowns or penetrations by the offense. This offensive advantage sometimes forces the defense to take on the zone principle until the defense forces stop the penetration, then quickly expand to flexible man-to-man assignments.

In all phases of team man-to-man fundamentals, stay away from zone principles as much as possible. *Man-to-man defense tools will not be perfected if you allow offensive pressure to push you into zone moves.*

The defense should have flexibility without shortchanging the team's complete intensity to get the job done. When the breakdown gives the offense an extra man, the remaining defense should stop the ball and disregard the man-to-man assignment. The balancing defender picks up the open man instantly.

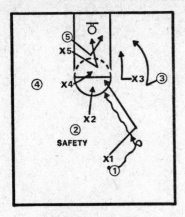

Diagram 9-22

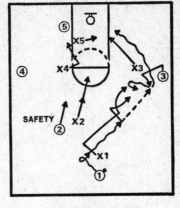

Diagram 9-23

Don't let any deviations interfere with your teaching the drive toward one hundred and ten percent effort in attaining your defensive goals.

Diagram 9-22. Playmaking dribbler goes right toward wing O3, reverses to drive into the key for the shot, or feed to the uncovered teammate if defense is caught out on opponents. This is countered by the team center drop.

X1 should give one hundred percent to get back into position before O1 gets to free-throw line. X2 should drop in quick and attack O1 if his man is not cutting. X4 should slide into key and still be able to pick up on assignment, if he comes in or gets back out on the pass. X3 drops away from O3 as dribbler O1 reverses direction and keeps in pass lane of assignment as he drops down. X5 should play above O5 and not let the ball come in as he crosses the key with O5. If O1 clears coming in, X5 should pick up O1 to pressure the shot and try to stay in the pass lane as he leaves O5 to make it difficult to pass-off.

Diagram 9-23. This illustrates a team defensive left side drop against penetration from the right side of floor. X1 covering the dribbler should drop instantly as O1 executes pass to O3. X3 takes baseline position leaving just the inside drive. X1 takes that lane away and gives X3 time to come in and maybe two-time. X2 drops fast from O2 to help close off the key. X4 does the same, still ready for O4 to cut.

If X3 allows O3 to drive to the baseline, it forces O5 to leave his

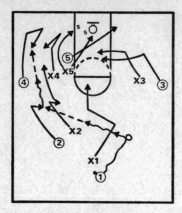

Diagram 9-24

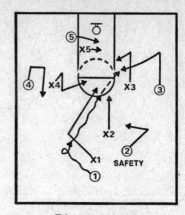

Diagram 9-25

under-the-basket assignment. X4 and X2 should come to pressure the pass-in to O5 and get rebound positions.

The following illustrations are samples of team drops to aid in shutting off penetration toward the key or penetrations that start from the corners.

Diagram 9-24. This diagram pictures the left side drop against penetration by O1 dribbling left toward wing O4, then reversing into the key. Weak-side X2 and X3 do the fast drop to defense key and stop O1 coming in, leaving O2 open. X3 will roll down with ballside position if O3 cuts for the basket. X4 drops to the key ready to pick up O4 if he cuts. O5, moving across the key, should be covered on ballside by X5. Don't let O5 receive a pass.

Diagram 9-25. This illustrates the flexible team key drop against the side baseline penetration attack. The offense sets O4 in corner with playmaker O2 setting in the wing spot. As O1 starts pass to O2, X1 should flash back into head of the key. As O2 passes to O4 in corner, X2 should flash to the key at medium post position. X5 ballside positions on O5. X4 should drive O4 up in order to get help from X2. If O5 rolls away, X3 from weak side will come in and cover. X5 should keep ballside position on O5 ready to stop dribbler O4. Also be ready to follow O5 halfway across the key. O3 will be left open momentarily.

10

Tools for Countering
Cutting over Screen Moves

This chapter deals with individual tools in man-to-man defense with team relationships to counter offensive cutting and screen moves.

COUNTERING KEY AREA SCREEN MOVES
BY OVER-THE-TOP FLEXIBLE MOVES

With the offense penetrating your defense to approximately 18 feet from the basket, your defensive move should come over the top of the screen to stop the 18 foot screen shot from going up without pressure. (At the college level the over-the-top tool would cover most of the half-court.) Your spacing is down to 2 to 3 feet due to the closeness of the basket. Your intensity at this moment should be the greatest. Strive to maintain that essential shoulder lead when coming up to the screen. Strive to push the running lane of the dribbler up away from the screen, and strive to get through fast. Release quickly a few inches as you pass the screen to gain back your spacing against the right-hand dribble and pressure out quickly. Stay low, bring hips forward, and take a long stride as you pass the screen, ready to release for position.

Remember, if a player's teammate makes a switch to stop the ball after a defensive player's error, the defender's drive for position should not let up. He should drive back between the screener and the basket to block the screener off. If the screener leaves sooner than the defender arrives, he should dive into the pass lane to block the roll-off pass. The defender guarding the screener should make a quick judgment and call a switch or stab as early as

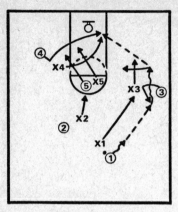
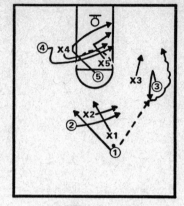

Diagram 10-1   Diagram 10-2

possible. The major error in making this move is to call for the switch too late. The flexible defense can position and space to eliminate the switching and keep away from mismatch weakness and board weakness.

Diagram 10-1. This illustrates screen and backdoor action away from the ball. O1 and O3 set up play by moving ball down the side away from screen action. O4 keeps time with the down move of O5 screen to cut across the key to the basket as O3 delivers the pass. Defender X4 guarding away from the ball should sink or drop to the key before the screen is set. X4 should get on top of the screen, thus forcing the one-way cut of O4. Then he should beat him across and down the key to a low post position. X5 should release and be ready to ballside O5 if he cuts to ball or basket. X1 and X2 drop deep to the key. X3 should play baseline position to try to force O3 to come into X1 and X2 drop-positions.

X4 should remember that O5 screen can be set low or high, and he should make the right flexible move to counter O4 play action and screen. X5 should keep in mind that he is the last pressure to apply to counter the play inside and back-boarding the shot. O4 lane is under the screen as a counter to over-the-screen action of X4.

Diagram 10-2. The cutter O4 goes over the top of screener O5. Flexible defensive moves are the same as the above explanation.

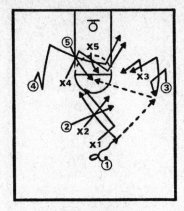

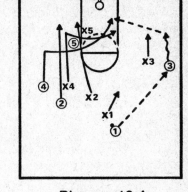

Diagram 10-3   Diagram 10-4

X4 should make his move according to a high or low screen set. Standard flex position can be on top of the screen to force backdoor. X5 releasing toward the ball and up from screener O5 giving X4 room to counter the cut. X5 should play the pass lane and be ready for any O5 post's move or cuts.

Diagram 10-3. This illustrates a slight floor position change of screen position and cutter. This deep screen set is the easiest to defend if X4 maintains top of screen position. The distance between baseline and screen is small, which makes it easy to beat cutter O4 across key to maintain ballside position. X5 should give X4 any lane he wishes to take to pick up cutting O4. X5 should be ready for center post move.

Diagram 10-4. This illustrates an explosive straight angle cut by O4 over the high post side screen. X4 should have space release at start and drive over the top of screen going to the low post basket corner. X4 should increase speed as he comes over O5 screen. X5 should release toward ball after X4 drops.

This gives X4 room to cut. O4 will cut off of O2 moving down to the basket. This deep angle cut depends upon speed and any slight hesitation by X4 as he moves down through the screens and maintains a ballside position to open the pass lane. X2 should lead O2 down through the screen O5. X2 should be ready for O2's cut to the basket, and should maintain the necessary ballside spacing.

ATTACKING OFFENSIVE ARC DRIVES

A common error made by many players is to follow the arc of the opponent's movement. Defending on an arc, the guard seems to get married to the opponent and he allows the dribbler to close the spacing. This gives the opponent an easy opportunity to turn his shoulder in, increase his speed, and take the defender right into the basket.

Drill the cut-across-the-arc defensive move to readjust position on every two or three dribbles, or steps, by the opponent. These straightline moves use the shortest distance between two points to counter the arc move of the opponent. Best position is square on the dribbler's ball.

This too should force the offensive player off the arc if your straightline man gains the lead-shoulder-ahead postion that could pressure him out. Players at all levels are caught on this move and allow opponents to score or foul them in the process. *Drill and drill and drill* this floor situation by chalking an arc on each side of the key. Have defenders execute the straightline cut-offs until they are overlearned.

Diagram 10-5. The following arc moves vary some on the start. The importance should be stressed of leading cutter on ballside, but never allowing the cutter to move into you when cutting hard for the basket. X3 should use the straight line move to be ahead of dribbler and pressure out to force a change in the dribble arc. This should be done at the shot positions O3 has developed on the arc.

Diagram 10-5

The emphasis here is placed on handling this offensive move, based on the number of times the defensive players are beaten by this move. One high school player developed two shots off this move and made the All State team. One Ohio State player averaged 29 points a game by developing three or four shots on the arc. The mechanics of the counter move can be taught as a defensive tool so the players do not rely on just reflex defense playing. Develop the right flexible habit, then the reflex for the situation can take over. By plotting the exact shot move on the arc and having the defender make his straight cut move to pressure a change of arc, he can throw off the shot rhythm.

Diagram 10-6. This pattern shows a circle offense moving counterclockwise after going clockwise. After the first pass from O1 to O2, O2 fakes the right side, reverses the ball counterclockwise, and passes to O3. O4 slides down to force X4 to move. O3, after the fake, flashes down through the key and around the screener O5. X3 should go with O3 maintaining a ballside position all the way down and through the key. The best defensive position for X3 would be to come up the key inside of screener O5 to take a ballside position as O3 comes up. X3 is in position to go down the key if O3 reverses back. X3 positions at the top of the screen and stops O3 from shooting in front of the screen. X5 should be loose and alert. Allow X3 full lane freedom but be ready for O5 to flash up for the ball. O4

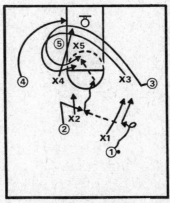

Diagram 10-6

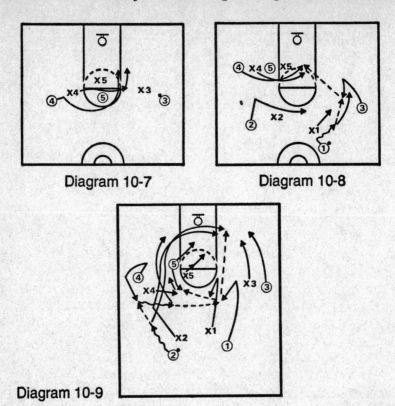

Diagram 10-7   Diagram 10-8

Diagram 10-9

uses screener O5 and moving screen O3 coming under the basket to receive the pass from O2.

Diagram 10-7. This illustrates the double pressure that is put on the defender in the fake back, up and over, high post screen. With the screen high, X4 can drop in toward the key below the screen which makes his defense of O4's backdoor move easy. With O3 and the ball at the extended free throw line, X4 is in a good position to slip the O5 screen. X5 should release back and toward the ball but he must not interfere with X4's moves. He must be ready for O5's movement toward the ball.

Diagram 10-8. X4 should not drop back in screener O5's lap. O4 wants X4 to go behind the screen. X4 should cut over for a ballside position. This drill gives X4 practice to come over the top and take a ballside position against O4 as he comes up. The frequent error by defender X4 is the failure to drop toward the key and to the top of the screen before he loses his spacing.

Diagram 10-9. This illustrates a double attack by O2 and O4. It starts as a left side attack with O2 setting up the give-and-go. He goes down through the low post and up to high post for a pass that can be fed by O4 or O1. O2 has a third move off the down-cut by a button-hook move as he reaches the low post position. X2 should angle position dribbler O2. At the pass to O4, X2 releases quickly back down toward the ball and maintains ballside position. X2 moves inside of O2 after he passes the ball, ready to come up through the key on ballside of O2.

COUNTERING WING POST SIDE SCREEN AND ROLL

Diagram 10-10. This illustrates the flexible defensive team play between X3 and X5. O3 is attempting to use O5 as a screen with O5 moving toward X3 then rolling to basket. Inside post when setting for a move toward wing, to screen and roll toward the basket, will try to embarrass the switch defense tool. The defender X3 against wing drive for the key should quickly release and move into the dribbler's running lane. This forces an early change of direction over the screen. The defender X3 releases as he passes the screen to get a proper position to contain O3's drive down into the key. The defender X5 against screener should give an early side screen warning. The screen defender X5 should be half fronting the screener to give him position to trap or fake at the dribbler and move down in passing lane as his assignment rolls toward the basket.

With O5 screener moving all the way out to O3, to screen, X5 follows out releasing space ready to jump the dribbler and roll with O5 to the basket. Suppose a last resort switch takes place, the

Diagram 10-10

defender X3 being screened, should release back as X5 calls "Screen!" If O5 leaves early X3 should cut the pass lane. X3 must come over O5 to eliminate the pass-off to O5. X5 should go for a trap before play can develop. Such a switch may put him in a mismatch situation. Drill to stop the screen without a switch.

Diagram 10-11. This illustrates the low post interchange with a moving screen by O5. Hesitating, X4 gives time for O4 to receive pass-in by O3. X4 watches out for the high or the low screen, and sets for O4 to receive pass-in by O3. X5 has two defensive moves that can be used. First, he may stay in the low post pass lane for two counts, then move, after screening O5; O5 would come to the ball or go up the key after moving from the screen to the post. X5 should keep ballside always. Second, X5 may take the lane pressure, go quickly with O5 but play him loose ballside, ready to go high if O5 moves up.

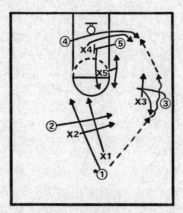

Diagram 10-11

ATTACKING WEAK-SIDE DOUBLE POST SCREEN

The position of the weak-side screens and the cutter off the screens will dictate the defender's position and movement to solve the problem with flexible tools. The low post screener's defender X5 should position above the screen toward the ball with good spacing. The top screener will take similar position, and both must be alert to give defender X2 of cutter O2 the free running lane.

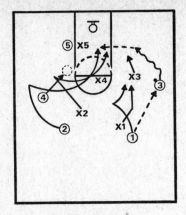

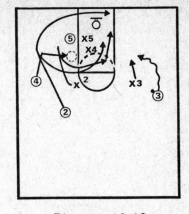

Diagram 10-12   Diagram 10-13

Diagram 10-12. The primary move by the offensive pattern will
be to tie up X2 on the double screen with O2 getting the pass; or
forcing a switch with O4; or O5 with the open screener on a switch
moving for the pass. A third cut would be by O5 coming up and
around O4 for a pass. This sometimes causes confusion with X4
moving around X5 to get position. X2 should remember that O2
has two lanes to use by taking top of screener O5's position. X2 has
eliminated the first threat with X2 ready to drive down to pressure
low post position if O2 goes backdoor.

Diagram 10-13. This is the toughest play for defender X2 to face.
With O2 outside and down to baseline, X2 should be down ready to
go through the key on the baseline if O2 breaks in that direction. If
O2 brings opponent X2 over halfway to the top post position then
starts either backdoor or over the top of screener O5, X2 should
release the maximum space to gain time to get over the screen. It is
best to go to position on top of high post ready to drive to the
baseline at corner of the basket. Or come over O5 with ballside
position on O2.

O2 may move in close to double screen before cutting high or
low. It is better to go over the top with help of X4 and X5, by
sliding down to stop the pass, if X2 is late.

Diagram 10-14. This illustrates the third move to trap X4 on the
strong side. O4 will bring X4 clear by screener O2, then reverse
over O2 toward the baseline corner. If X4 is caught, O3 will throw
a looping pass to O2. If X4 is late, O4 will shoot or drive for a shot.

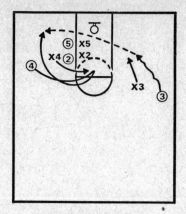

Diagram 10-14

X4 should position to stop a baseline dribble drive. It is of the greatest importance that screen defender X2 has released some spacing to give X4 a chance to move through. X2 is talking X4 through, ready to pick up any O2 move toward the ball.

FORCING VERTICAL MEDIUM POST WING-SIDE SCREEN AND ROLL

Diagram 10-15. The vertical pick-and-roll is one of the most difficult defensive problems to solve, especially if it is set up to get screen shot in the sixty percent shooting area. You should play your dribbler loose. He has two ways to go and shutting off one move is

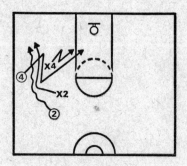

Diagram 10-15

not the answer. With team talk you know the position of rear screen. Start your dribbler on the angle and get position at the first or second dribble to force him out away from screen. If you get too close when forcing, release with banana move after you have passed screen.

One of the most common failures to stop a screen attack is failure of the player being screened to get an early release of additional inches in spacing to give him extra time to defeat the screen situation. When defender's opponent attempts to walk him into the screen, he should execute a quick jump release to the top of the screen. He should also keep the ballside position clear to low post if the cutter backdoors.

The medium screen set halfway between sideline and key with the dribbler starting in front and above the screen creates a vertical action with the dribbler driving by or passing to post. This is followed by offensive dribbler or player to cut hard down over the screen on the way to the basket.

If you are caught standing when your opponent starts don't expect to beat him. The defender's first move is to break the dribbler or the passer off the vertical lane cut and force him to angle out. This must be done *away* from the screen *not near it*. The offensive movement is a hard down court drive outside the screen. By jumping his running lane after first dribble you take away the main threat and force him to a secondary inside move.

You must now contend with the reverse dribble by releasing away from the dribbler. Shoot ahead of the moving player before attempting to pressure again. Your last resort is to switch. That may make a mismatch even if you are successful in changing opponents. Over-learn all other defensive tools before using the switch as a last chance defense.

Remember the most important counter move to nullify the dribbler's threat of gaining position by reverse, back dribble, fake reverse, and change of pace, *is space releasing*. Releasing back away from the move to gain more spacing inches gives you the time to blunt his true action.

The best move you can make against all screens is the release of inches back at oncoming screen and then move 4 to 6 inches left back to right, or right to left.

COUNTERING SHUFFLE AND PASSING GAME PATTERNS

In all patterns the strength of the opponents can be offset by the defense if its performance is just as dedicated and over-learned as the offense. Every player must have the same learning experience with his opponent working from each position. This *countering flexible defense must maintain a constant ballside position*. Generally a thoroughly disciplined pattern with good speed tempo will begin to penetrate the defense by the time the pattern goes into the third flip-flop.

The weakest defender may get careless in reading the move of his opponent cutting to the next station. Or he may get mechanical and miss the opponent changing the pattern.

The weakness of the pattern is a result of its strength. There are few opportunity check moves off a disciplined pattern. If a well-grooved defense can equal or quicken the tempo of the motion, the offensive pattern will be countered. Another result of the pattern is the use of time the ball remains in their hands. Both teams must concentrate on no turnovers or fouls.

Every defender should play loose ballside and run in the running lanes of the offensive man and contest every pass lane. This will result in a slowdown of the pattern's tempo.

The defense must also put great pressure on the passing points of the pattern. *Force them to move*. Don't follow their tempo. Be quicker. Hold ball position and contest every pass lane. *Never take your eye completely off opponent or ball*. If a penetration occurs, the defense should collapse fast to the inside and hard to the board. Remember their patience will try to lull you to sleep or make you take wild chances. Spacing must be corrected at all times and defender should never lose ballside position. The defender should be alert to anticipate the next move. Defender should talk to teammates as they slip the top of screens. He should never take his eyes completely off his man. *Be sure of ball vision*. Defender must keep in continuous motion to make it harder for screen to find him.

Shuffle Game Multiple Screens
Team Moves and Counters

Diagram 10-16. Drill at a jog pace to get acquainted with the moves, then increase tempo to game speed. Be sure to show some

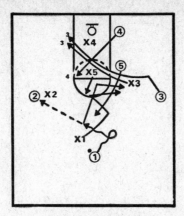

Diagram 10-16

alternate moves off the pattern 10-16, in order for the defense to be alert for the moves, not just locked into the basic move. Remember to concentrate on stopping the ball movement by the end of the second time through. The third time through, the motion frequently breaks free for a shot, generally a short inside shot. During the third move the defenders should call upon all their concentration and intensity. My experience with the motion indicates that forcing to the fourth move favors the defense most of the time.

The diagram illustrates the patterns of the first movements of the shuffle game. The pattern will use counters off the basic move in order to keep the defense honest. O1 brings the ball up on the strong side to pull the defender into O3. O1 passes to the weak-side O2 with O3 going over the screen O5. O4 breaks toward O2 from low post to high post cutting just back of O3 as he cuts through. O1 passing to O2 cuts down to set high screen to allow post screener O5 to come out ready to receive a pass from O2. O1, after the screen, cuts to sideline ready to receive pass from O5. As the pass starts to side wing O1, O2 cuts over the top of the screen with low post O3 coming up across the key to the ball. This movement can be continuous.

Passing Game Defense

Diagram 10-17. This shows offensive players' moves with specific spots numbered. Each move of pattern shows where each player should go. Follow the numbers.

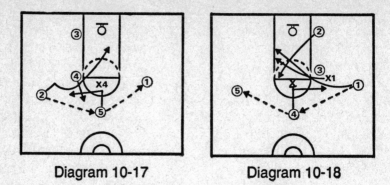

Diagram 10-17   Diagram 10-18

The first defensive pressure is X1 forcing dribbler O1 to go to the strong side. The ball should be on the weak side to make use of cutters over the double screen. With pass going to O2, X2 should move in and force the pass. At times he may drop back into the pass lane to put on lane pressure. As O3 cuts down over double screen or backdoors the screens, X3 should release to the top of the screen to beat O3 over. Or cut down key if O3 backdoors.

X4 has the toughest problem with O4 timing the cutting up over moving screen O3. X4 should release up the key and be in cutter's O4 lane to keep position as O4 comes up across key to high post. X1 should release back into key on the pass O1 to O2. O1 passes and cuts down to top screen X5. X5 should come out on ballside and make return pass to O5 difficult. X5 should force O5 out of position. X1 keeps ballside position ready to cut out as O1 goes to wing position away from ball. With the O2 pass to point O5 who passes to the opposite wing, O1, the pattern moves begin again with all five offensive men starting from different positions. It is absolutely necessary that each defender practices the flexible defensive moves from each pattern position. Defense should release and protect the inside. Talk! Talk! Talk! This is a big help. Put pressure on the wing playmakers at all times.

Diagram 10-18. At this point pattern starts the third motion. The diagram pictures positions of the numbered players after their third complete movement. This offense is highly structured and calls for great discipline and high team passing ability. To be successful the pattern should run at a good tempo. Defensive players should talk! talk! and hustle over the screens. Defenders should time coming from low post to high. Defender of point wants to fight

to keep ball from going to the weak side. Don't take your eyes off
your assignment, he may break the pattern to receive ball and
shoot. Defender of weak side wing O5 needs to close in and force
him to move to spoil timing with cutter.

Diagram 10-19. This illustrates a double post screen roll-out on
each side of the key. O1, the playmaker, works the ball at the point
position. The screen down from the wings should time with the
point man's ball moving. The pattern is always ready to take advantage of a defender who gets caught on a screen. The baseline drive
is always there, and the pass into the inside post with the passer as
a cutter. Add the weakside wing cutting over or back of inside
screen. The inside screen moves under, screening for opposite
screen coming over. The pass pattern keeps the total defense busy.
It pulls the best rebounders away from the basket at times; it
attacks both sides of the defense quickly; it has several alternate
moves such as hitting inside post with backdoor and weak-side
action. Defenders X4 and X5 should go out on the baseline side of
the wings, O2 and O3, screening down. They should position to
stop the baseline drive while pressuring the post now playing wing.
O1 and O2 will interchange at times if both are good playmakers.
O2 reverses away from the ball and moves down to screen O4. O2
moves to the ball and becomes point man.

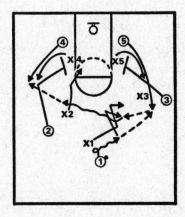

Diagram 10-19

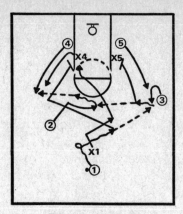

Diagram 10-20

Diagram 10-20. O1 and O2 will interchange at times if both are good playmakers. All defenders should be able to play good post defense. With the in-and-out screen play executed by O3 and O5 weak side, X2 and X4 should release toward the strong side. X1 should pressure O1 and pass lanes and be aware of the give-and-go opportunity of O1.

11

Countering Fast Breaks,
Control Patterns,
and Out-of-Bounds Plays

Flexible positioning applies pressures in several areas whose objective is limiting, slowing down, or stopping the fast break.

To build a good fast break you should know every possible defense the opposition coaches will throw against it.

There is the breakaway attack, releasing one man on the shot. This can come from any defense. Man-to-man defense can be your defense for stopping many break moves.

In your pattern attack you should designate and practice with one guard or outside man staying in a good defensive position. His job is to help the ball handler to penetrate the defense for a good shot. Good teams will have one or two men retreating and three moving in to pressure the rebound as the shot goes up.

AREAS FOR PRESSURING FAST BREAK DEVELOPMENT

Some coaches feel, for good reasons, that the break should be stopped first on the board by tying up the rebounder and forcing him to dribble out of pressure. The major key for break success is to get the quick pass to the outlet man. Slowing down that pass enables three men to be back on defense slowing or stopping the break move. First man back on defense covers the long bomb pass. A late release to the defense will hurt the defense.

Other coaches feel that their teams will handle the offensive boards. They develop a five-man rotating pattern. But some shots

185

taken could catch the two best defensive players out of position. Defensively speaking it would be sounder to have one of the key defensive players in a position to cover the back court *fast*. I prefer two defenders. One, long; the second, at free throw line ready for the break out. The third man away fast from rebound releases back as the number three defender. Three defenders can slow the break.

Second, other coaches will try to pressure the outlet man at the side court. But to be successful this takes defensive timing, or it takes help from the offense throwing the outlet pass mechanically, or if the offense fails to see other open pass lanes. The further down court the outlet pass, the easier it is to intercept. But if it is completed the break is much faster.

If your outlet pressure and board pressure forces the outlet to come back past the head of the key for the ball, you have practically taken the fast break away. Quickness of the pass and delivery is of equal importance along with the accuracy of the pass.

The third place to slow up the break is the slowing down of the dribbler as he goes down the sideline or center court. You should pyramid your defense at the ball point. The sideline dribble cuts down the defense court coverage and the middle drive forces you to split your forces to either side, or both at the same time. At release from basket the defense is wise to stack the middle and force break always to the side of court.

Your players should realize that it is every defensive man's responsibility to help slow the dribbler.

The fourth place to stop the break is to drop back ahead of the ball with an equal number of defense men to match the offensive thrust. This means that at the loss of the ball position in rebounding, you release quickly by flashing back with three fast and accelerating steps. This flash back on defense should put you even or ahead of the ball.

Some coaches, to stop the break, will try to get two offensive men to go up with the rebounder, one on each side, then come down with him to tie up the ball and his hands. If you miss tying up the ball, the offense has a four or three break.

St. Louis University played the famous Kentucky University fast break team a few years ago. St. Louis was a well-disciplined controlled basketball team. They had an excellent defensive re-

bounder at center who held most of the opponent's offensive rebounding to one shot. St. Louis worked on the control plan all
during the season to move and screen until one player got a non-
pressure shot from the sixty percent shooting area or better. As the
shot was taken, all five men drove back down the floor and tightly
set their defense in front of the Kentucky whirlwind. Ball control
for two or three minutes created havoc with Kentucky and they
made defensive errors. The St. Louis center stayed under the
basket four or five times during the game, got two goals and tipped
three clear out to his retreating team. The Kentucky team hit for a
poor percentage, shooting mostly from the outside. They were
worrying about how the first shot must go down or they would lose
the ball. This strategy beat a great Kentucky National Champion-
ship team.

Another strategy used by many teams is to fight fire with fire:
break back against the break as fast as it comes down. *Unless your
break is your major weapon and equal to your opponent's, it would
be folly to use a secondary offense against an opponent's basic
offensive attack.*

A fast transition defense is one counter we used successfully to
stop opponent's break and give us a run of points. At the instant
loss of the ball, or when the ball goes through the basket, the
defense flashes to positions ahead of the key ready to point out
their assignments, and to build flexible defensive power in front of
the ball and to fight it all the way back.

A defense that is well-organized and well-knit is tough to move
on, even from the three-fourth court on back. Remember that you
cannot always match up against teams that throw different men
down court. Your deep defense should cover any who come and
then switch back assignment at the earliest opportunity. This same
procedure is used in executing a switching defense.

The break defense should stop the fast break at the start or beat
it down court with equal number of defensive players in position to
stop any penetration.

POSITIONING TO PRESSURE THE FAST BREAK

Some defensive break pressures upset the rhythm and tempo of
a fast break team beyond the specific floor pressure areas.

A controlled basic pattern run for a long period of time will take the break feel away from some teams. Sometimes a surprise break run right back at the breaking team, providing it is well executed, will embarrass and tighten up the fast break team when their score is matched immediately at the opposite end of the floor.

Diagram 11-1. This shows some of the areas where the fast break pressures are applied. Defensive positioning in the number one area is used by many coaches. You need to decide which defensive form to use to put slow-down pressure on the offensive break pattern.

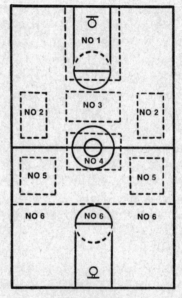

Diagram 11-1

No. 1 Area—Board Pressure. If you have a board advantage in height and spring, by all your men, use it to the hilt. Sometimes by putting two rebounders to drive on the ball going up with offense and pressuring the ball all the way to the floor can slow down the outlet pass. Screening the ball and vision of offensive rebounder may force him to dribble out. Don't waste defensive power by trying the board pressure if the opponent has the advantage. Sometimes the defense can get enough of the rebound to tip it out regardless of coverage.

No. 2—Outlet Pressure. In dropping back one defender flares out into the No. 2 area playing the man and ball going for an interception. Most coaches like to build all the defensive power possible in the center court lane by using one man on the ball all the way. It is dangerous with the outside or sideline pressure move. A good break could fake you and be on the way by passing over or by using another pass lane. A clever flexible defender times his move out as the pass starts. Remember *the longer the pass the faster the break, but also the longer pass CAN be intercepted.*

No. 3—Pass Lane Pressure and Slow Down. This area is the first fall back area for establishing a coordinated flexible defense. The fast break generally runs in three lanes—the middle and both sidelines. This is your first team pressure to force and keep ball out of the middle. Such a defensive move forces the fast break to one side of floor. Flexible defense tries to keep on one side, cutting down the fast break to less than fifty percent of its potential. Pick up the center cutter and go with the ball side all the way.

No. 4—Team Pressures on Dribbler. The center-of-court ten-second line pressure many times will force pressure areas at this point. Slow down the dribbler, force him into errors. There is a chance of two-timing the offensive man with the ball. He has not penetrated deep enough to set patterns.

No. 5—Keep Ball on Sideline Pressure. The two ten-second corners are ideal places to force ball to the sidelines. You are cutting fifty percent of his pass lanes. Your total team defense shifts to the right or left side on the ball using it as the point for our perimeter defense set on closing inside pass lanes.

No. 6—All Defense Stop Penetration Area. This area is our high pressure flexible defense working at its best—offensive defense attacking aggressively to shut off close shots and get ball in the shortest time. The fast break at this point should try to put ball up quickly with a non-pressure shot. The break to delay has a devastating effect on the break game tempo, if the break wants 75 to 100 shots a game. If defense has just two defenders down in front of ball, they need to play the overload in a vertical position—top man stopping the ball to force side pass then dropping to basket fast as low man moves to press ball. Third man back picks up point.

POSITIONING TO PRESSURE CONTROL PATTERNS

If your team is going to force the opposition into a turnover, all five of your men must be pressuring the ball and pass lanes besides executing change of positions *fast*. Defense cannot over-shift to the outside and stop the oppositions' inside moves toward the basket.

Each defensive man should be synchronized with his opponent with shoulder ahead ballside coming out from the basket—always looking for backdoor plays. Have just enough spacing to hand pressure pass lane but with controlled movement to stop the backdoor move.

If the ball goes into the middle, the perimeter defenders sink toward the middle. *Wing men* move out to *pressure* as their assignment moves away from the basket. Defender sinks to inside just enough to stop the ball but should always be ready to pressure his assignment if the ball comes back out. Hand pressuring the pass lane, be sure your released spacing away from your opponent will allow you to stop the reverse or backdoor move. When taking your sink steps, leave part of pass lane open to bait your opponents into trying to force it through.

Many defenders exaggerate their sinks to help to stop inside penetration only to be completely out of position to press the ball as their opponent receives it.

To defeat the ball control of your opponents, your team must be in better condition and use a faster tempo. Your team should be well versed on the ball control pattern to make the right moves to allow them to double-pressure the ball and the passing lanes. Two-time opportunity comes by forcing the ball toward a teammate so his move is short and quick with opportunity to get back an assignment.

Remember, your strategy is to move men faster than the ball can be passed. Possibly it will be an error on the part of the control people that will lead the defense to gain possession of the ball. This is a result of sufficient pressure.

If closing game-time dictates a foul for possession, foul the poorest shooter or the least experienced player. The defender keeps the pass lanes covered as he moves towards the ball, thus causing the loop pass to be thrown. This helps teammates in their drive for interceptions. Expert dribblers are hard to stop without fouling. The defenders should two-time before dribbler starts or at the time he stops, also in a slowdown move. As he moves the ball the second defender should try to come up on blind side of the dribbler at the same time that his teammate pressures the dribbler's movement with a frontal attack.

Another defense tool is to place your second best pressure man on this dribbler to try to keep the ball out of his hands. If your number two man can do this successfully, it leaves the number one defender to work on lesser ball handlers.

Another point for applying the tying-up or ball-stealing pressure is to force the dribbler to move close to a second defender for two-timing.

To leave a player wide open to run for a two-time situation is a waste of energy and also costly. If the pattern is scattered over the half court, the one covering should be good enough to cause the opponent with the ball to dribble. Try to stay on the seconds needed for a held ball result.

If opponents use an expanded fast ball handling drive and screen pattern, the defense should execute a faster tempo to apply the same pressure that took place in defending the regular pattern positions. The defenders will be covering more space than before. Your flex spacing should consider the extra distance from basket.

If you use one big defender to move from side baseline pressure to guard the key before the ball arrives, then at the instant the ball starts inside a topside defender should drop back and cover the side opponents, especially the side left by the big man. This should give a one-on-one match up. At the time the ball breaks inside the perimeter, a close outside defender can flash in to quick two-time the move if possible.

When the defense men two-time they should get in position at the same time and force a pass to come up over their heads. Remember, if you allow the dribbler to split the two-time and break toward center court, the defense pressure is defeated. Three defenders against five offensive players.

BALL CONTROL PATTERNS

The remaining three defenders must instantly take position on the pass lanes of the three closest opponents and force the longest pass. Leave the lane slightly open to the passer in order to sucker the pass to a teammate who is partially covered. This makes possible the interception by quick decision-making or the go-for-ball reaction.

Generally ball control is put on for a *short period* which helps eliminate some possible turnovers by the ball control attack. A ball control pattern away from the basket is used most of the time by a team that is ahead or a speed team who lacks height trying to free the key lane from defense, or a team killing the clock at half time or end of the game. It has a drive potential for the basket.

Delayed pattern offenses give a change of pace on the attack, drawing defenses away from the basket, giving more room for cutters to shake loose for passes. Done properly they will change the game tempo, work the time down on the clock, and be frustrating to the team that needs the ball along with a fast game tempo. Such a control game has a constant scoring threat by reversing directions, by cutting off screen position, and by cutting receiving passes from high post.

Diagram 11-2. This illustrates the two-one-two ball control pattern setting up near ten-second line, thus drawing the defense away from the basket. Inside O5 sets up above the key moving laterally and is always a threat to cut for the basket. O2 moves down to set a screen on X4 to release O4 to come up and receive the first pass from dribbler O1.

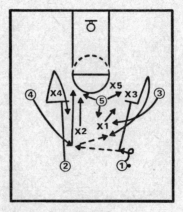

Diagram 11-2

O1 and O2, going down to let O4 and O3, come up for the ball and may break off the screen, cutting for the basket. O4 and O3 pass and cut down to screen for O1 and O2. The ball can be passed into O5, who feeds the cutter or goes to the basket. O5 also acts as a safety for a teammate by moving out for a pass. X1 and X2 should keep ballside position and be alert to cover O1 and O2 in case they break for the basket off the screens. X5 should keep ballside as the ball changes sides. X4 and X3 should slide inside the screens coming up with assignments. This pattern can move the ball fast and continuously. The wings and screeners will vary their distance from the side, changing pass lanes to make it tougher to defend. The offensive outside passing weave's good points are constant motion of the perimeter play with hard cutters around high post O5 who also acts as a safety valve and as a third cutter. By keeping this weave out toward the ten-second line, with a lead, the offense forces the defense to cover a greater area. The offense still has basket scoring drive and ball control which pressures the defense into gambling if it is not patient.

Diagram 11-3. This illustrates the basic set and the first and second moves. As O1 brings the ball into position to attack, O2 and O4 interchange to clear O4 for the first pass. O1 goes down over the top of the screen O5, rolling right to take O3's position as O3 moves to the top. O4 passing to O3 cuts down on either side of screener O5 and turns left to take O3's position.

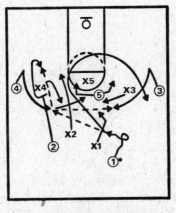

Diagram 11-3

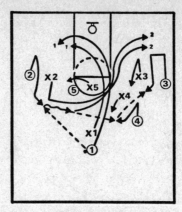

Diagram 11-4

Diagram 11-4. This shows the position changes after the first move. Defender X1 should release fast to the front of screener O5. This allows X1 to cut off the drive of O1 in either direction. Ballside is the position. X4 should release to the inside to eliminate O2 who screens down. X2 should be alert for O2 to cut off screen as the pass might go to screener O5. X3 going away from the ball should sink inside but play even with O3. Be alert for a backdoor. X4 should be alert for O4 exploding down over O5 as the second cutter.

BASELINE OUT-OF-BOUNDS PLAYS

These plays are set up to try for a score or for an entry into regular patterns without losing too much time. Generally they attempt to screen for one best shooter to free him to shoot from his best position. If possible the plays try for the close-in shot. The defense should play loose with ballside position to protect the basket and the key area.

Some teams zone such plays to eliminate the screen. It is possible to pick this zone by keeping a player from defending his area. If the zone faces the ball and does not see the player movement it will allow penetration. Players cannot stand in a zone and be successful.

Diagram 11-5. The baseline out-of-bounds pattern emphasizes a set for the tall post near the basket, ready to take the high toss. X1 and X2 work their defense tight to the post to limit his ability to move. X1 will stop the post O5 from moving to the basket. X2 will

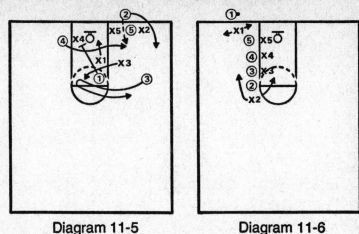

Diagram 11-5   Diagram 11-6

stop the movement out and play in front until the pass starts in. If the pass goes outside, X2 should pick his assignment O2. X5 and X3 should stay in tight until the pass starts, then pick up their assignments. This stops post O1 from fading back for a pass. X4 stays inside of wide O4 and away from the ball position that O4 takes. O1 drops down to top pick X4. X4 should release up toward O1 before the screen gets in to allow him room to stop the play.

Diagram 11-6. The Vertical Alignment throws up a wall with three or four variations of players breaking from the pattern. The defense's first objective is to cut off the inside move and the pass. You can use a straight zone defense. I prefer the combination of partial zone and flexible man-to-man. First, shut off the pass to baseline post with X1 positioning in tight ballside against O5. X1 is also responsible for O1 after he passes and steps inside. X4 stays man-to-man on O4. X2 and X3 will take either O2 or O3 whichever breaks in their direction.

Diagram 11-7. This pattern illustrates the horizontal free-throw line set which emphasizes screening for a key shot artist. If O5 or O3 drops behind the three-man screen, X5 or X3 will follow him back and force him to move. If O4 or O3 steps back, X4 or X3 should follow him closely through the vacated spot. X1 may play passer tight or loose in playing the pass lanes. If O5 and O2 flare to outside, X4 and X3 will pick them up. If O5 cuts inside, X5 will play him ballside to the basket. If X5 and X2 switch, both get back on assignments quickly.

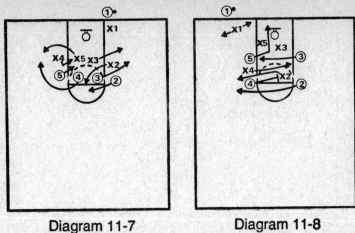

Diagram 11-7   Diagram 11-8

Diagram 11-8. This diamond pattern illustrates the angle double scissor movement. The toughest defense assignment is to stop the big post O5 who screens X3 as O3 rolls to the outside toward the ball. O5, having position on X3, steps toward the ball and the basket for the pass. Each pattern always has two or more moves to make. Again X1 can play ballside on O5's lap or tighten up on out-of-bounds' passers.

X5 should take the baseline move away from O5. X3 and X2 should play loose toward ballside to get enough spacing to sift through the screen. If the defense tries an over-the-top of the screen, the offense will move down the key to the basket. To help the slip, set high and loose on the man. This forces the screen to come higher to set effective lateral screens. Slipping the screen cuts off the screener's attempt to come through the middle of the key.

You should emphasize that talking is a most important defensive factor against these out-of-bound plays. Your defense should move quickly to ballside loose positions. They should never get caught tight. Talking always helps against any new position changes.

Your fundamental rule should be observed by all defenders: *Get and maintain ballside positions to force the pass out.*

Diagram 11-9 illustrates one out-of-bounds play from the box left set. The first objective of out-of-bounds play is to get inside to the big man O5. The second objective is to screen for the top outside shooter. Try to free him in his high percentage shot areas.

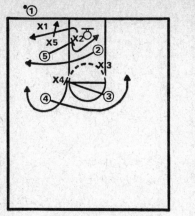

Diagram 11-9

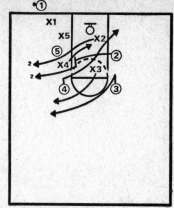

Diagram 11-10

O5 should be fronted by X1 or X5. X2 should slip the screen by playing released down from O2. X2 should jump O2's running lane. X1 has the key moves to execute. He should play on the baseline in the pass lane leading under the basket, ready to step into O5's pass lane. If O5 moves toward the sideline, X5 will follow him out. X5 should have the lane to stop O5 from getting the pass coming inside. X1 should flex to allow the X5 move. O4 and O3 criss-cross at the head of the key. X4 and X3 should play loose and slip the screen. If X2 is caught, X5 should protect the baseline outside of the box.

Diagram 11-10. This play changes the box position to change the screen angles and cuts. X1 still fronts O5 and forces him to move besides picking up O1 as he comes in court. X2 sees screen potential and should position to get over the top with O2.

Diagram 11-11. This play uses the front line of the box to screen with O4 and O5 cutting for the basket. X1 protects inside pass lane. X3 should have a ballside position on screener O3. X4 releases O4 toward the basket ready to take O4, cutting off the screen. O3 will come off the screen going to open spot as a safety.

Diagram 11-12. This play illustrates a three-man front near the baseline in order to hamper the defender's movements. X1, X5, and X3 should switch against any criss-cross on the front line. If one offensive player pulls out away from the ball or the basket, the defender should move out with him. X2 covering the outside man should go with him and call out if he screens. If O3 pulls out behind

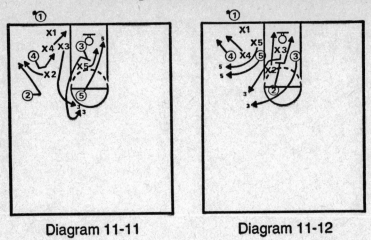

Diagram 11-11   Diagram 11-12

screener O2, X3 should pick screener O2. X4 picks up O3 coming out. Flexing X4 should pick O2 if he moves toward left sidelines. X2 switches to O3 coming out.

SIDELINE AT HEAD OF KEY

Diagram 11-13. This out-of-bounds play combines the cutters going off the screens, reversing the ball to the weak side, and moving into the opposition's general planning defense. O4 takes the out-of-bounds. O2 breaks down, giving O1 a moving screen to clear him for a pass. O2 sets screen on O3. O5, setting in behind defender X4, steps up and screens X4, allowing him to cut for the basket by using either inside or outside lane. When defense collapses inside, O4 will use the alternate pass lane to O5, as he steps into pass lane position. O4 then drives by O5 receiving a hand-off pass.

The defense of the sideline play should have ballside positions against their assignments. They should release sufficient space to break through the screens without losing position. X4 should play loose and see near screen O5. Teammate X5 must talk. X2 should go down ballside with O2 talking. X1 should be playing above opponent toward the ball. O2 continues down, screening X3, to give O3 a chance to get open for a pass. If O1 cannot pass inside, the pass will go to O3 who is released by a screen. O3 in turn will pass to O4 coming out from under the basket. X5 can drop off and

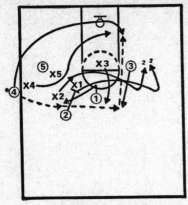

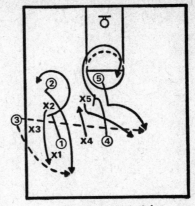

Diagram 11-13   **Diagram 11-14**

pressure pass lanes. It is best for X5 to stay on his opponent if he breaks. Remember X5 can follow O5 to the basket, or set a post ballside. O5, if he breaks, gets a pass from O1. Team defense should put pressure on their opponents who are moving away from the basket.

Diagram 11-14. This illustrates the sideline out-of-bounds play that starts at the defensive end of the court and forces the defense to cover the full court if the defense is pressing the ball. The play drives cutters O2 and O5 over screens for a long pass, with screeners cutting to open spots and acting as safety pass receivers. O3 should be a good passer with judgment to hit the open man. O2 and O5 basically cut hard for the basket to receive a long pass. Screeners O1 and O4 will roll off the screens to drive for open pass lanes. O1 may trail O2 or cut for an open safety valve pass lane. Again the defenders should maintain a ballside position and have sufficient spacing to counter the screen and break action. X3 should be careful to release back toward the basket as the pass starts in, if he wants to successfully counter as O3 cuts up the court. Defenders can pressure the offense hard if their opponents are moving away from the basket. Defenders should all be ready for a sprint, because that is the only way they will stop the long pass, which if completed means two points. Again they should talk and talk. X1 and X4 release and keep moving to spoil screen timing.

Some coaches will use the out-of-bounds under the basket on the sidelines and add a new move to cover the side situation. If game time and the score forces the defenders to a pressure play, they should use the faster out-of-bounds play. To cover a long pass up court, X3 plays down toward the basket to eliminate the give-and-go to O3. The defenders cover hard ballside to force the pass back if at all possible.

12

Flexible Defense Against Weave and Stack Patterns

PRESSURING THE WEAVE WITH FLEXIBLE POSITIONING

The three-man weave can present real problems for the defense if the weave is disciplined to maintain spacing distances, good tempo, timed hand-offs, and inside loops, and continues to pressure push the defense back to make possible some easy screen shots.

Diagram 12-1. The flexible team defense needs all of their team tools to counter this weave pattern. It takes great discipline to keep perfect position and spacing as the defense moves through the offensive weave.

The defender should have perfect position coming into and away from the ball.

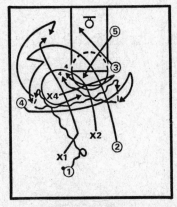

Diagram 12-1

X2 should have ballside position leading O2 to the baseline corner. X2 should keep the baseline cutting lane of O2 closed as the dribbler brings the ball down to the first hand-off position. X4 will position ballside of O4 as he moves across the key before dribbler O1 comes down with the ball. X1 should keep the right spacing going down with O1, and give X2 the right of way as O2 comes over the dribbler's screen.

X2 should have his shoulders ahead of O2 as the ball is handed off. If he stops just back of dribbler O1, he will be picked off, or allow O2 to beat him inside, or leave pass lane open to inside posts. As O2 brings ball over the top of the key, X4 should be positioned with shoulder leading as he goes past the hand-off by O2.

The one defensive weakness to strengthen is the acceleration move past the screen. Just a slight relaxing will burn the defender. X5 and X3 should have the spacing to ballside against the inside posts as the dribblers move the ball. At the instant any phase of the weave breaks through the defense, outside perimeter's defenders drop to the key to close off further penetration, and then pick up assignments quickly.

Diagram 12-2. This illustrates the O1 entry by picking up the wing O4 with his dribble hand-off. O1 could break toward O2 and start the weave in front of the key. The diagram shows the running lanes of X1, X4, and X2, and the slip through of the dribble hand-offs. On the second hand-off, O5 breaks to the post to receive a pass

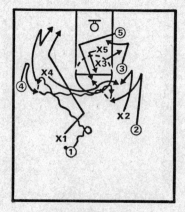

Diagram 12-2

from O2. Defenders X1 and X3 should be alert to O1 and O3 cutting for the basket.

Diagram 12-3. This shows a passing entry from O2 to O3 who may start the weave going down to pick up O1, or move up and in to pick up O2 who broke away to the opposite side of the key.

This changes the attack slightly by dribbler O2 making a pass entry to O3. O3 may reverse and go down to pick O1, or drive over the key and pick O2 who drove down the strong side ready to fake and come back over the ball. O4 and O5 have reversed positions going across the key toward the ball looking for a feed from dribbler O3, or from the hand-off receiver O1. O1 may continue weave by coming up over the key looking for O2 to come back up over the hand-off position.

Coaches *must* caution the defender of the dribbler to keep his spacing position to allow his teammate to slip quickly through the hand-off screen. If there is hesitation by the offensive man as he receives hand-off, at this time the defender should look out for reverse. The best flexible defense is through the screen ahead of the receiver, to stop an inside dribble drive.

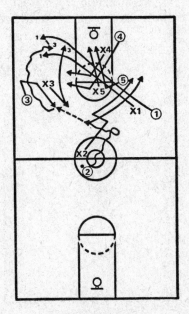

Diagram 12-3

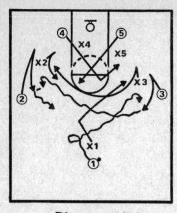

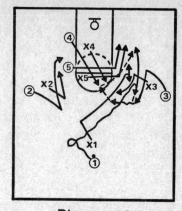

Diagram 12-4   Diagram 12-5

Diagram 12-4. This diagram illustrates the three-man weave with hand-offs moved closer to the head of the key in order to hit posts or get vertical cuts at the basket. The inside posts O4 and O5 criss-cross. They time their cuts with the hand-off from dribbler to outside man coming up over the dribbler's screen. X1 should hold baseline position in order to stop a fake hand-off and a continued drive for the basket. X1 should also hold sufficient spacing to allow his teammate X3 to come through unmolested. Again the most frequent error by defenders is to tighten up on the dribbler opponent as he moves up court. Keep inside pass lanes pressured and be ready for backdoor directional changes.

Diagram 12-5. The set of the weave is similar to O4, O5 at the side of the key. O5 crosses the key toward the ball and clears down for O4 to come to high post to receive a pass from O3. O2 starts his usual move then flashes a backdoor reverse as the ball comes to O4. This keeps the defense honest and not overplaying the outside man coming toward the ball. X4 should be alert for this move and beat his opponent up with a ballside position. *His flexible spacing is the answer.* X2 is the key to counter the sudden shift from the weave lanes. Again X2 spaces, dropping toward the key. X2 should keep his eye on his man all the time and not anticipate his movement toward the usual roll with O3.

Diagram 12-6. This illustrates reversing on the weave hand-off. Hand-off O1 continues to the basket with the receiver reversing to go to the basket outside of O1. This is a good move to counter

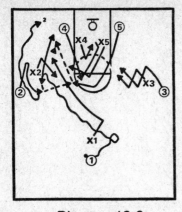

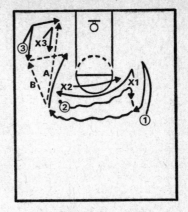

Diagram 12-6   Diagram 12-7

defensive switch at the hand-off point. O4 moves to the top of the key and away from the ball with O5 coming up for a pass and a hand-off. Defensive players must not get mechanical after the offense's first weave. The result will be to get burned with alternate moves. O2 passes inside or takes the reversed dribble. Play honest. Keep the pressure on the weave to hurt the opponents' opportunity to hit inside posts with passes.

Diagram 12-7. Most weaves do not have the variations to keep the defense honest. Actually the weave fakes the defense in and high, allowing the back-door variations to get free. This diagram illustrates the give-and-go in place of the side weave. If X3 tries to move up into the pass lane, (a) O3 will drive to the baseline for an inside shot. The weave defenders, X2 and X1, still play the same position and spacing. If the defense intends to switch or to two-time, this move is devastating. (b) A second move has give-and-go of O2 to O3 to split defense.

Diagram 12-8. This illustrates the variation of a weave called the wing fake-up and backdoor. The offense runs the weave two or three times just to suck X1 up ahead of O1 to anticipate the weave hand-off, and bang! goes the backdoor play. The above variations of the weave pattern take the pressure off the dribblers and the hand-offs. They also open up the inside pass lanes to the posts with at least two cutters going to the basket on the inside passes. This is tough to defense. The tempo is sharp but under control. If you have gamblers playing defense: LOOK OUT!

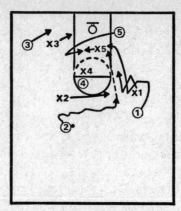

Diagram 12-8

The hand-off spots should be about 20 to 25 feet apart to give the dribbler a good passing angle to use in passing to the inside posts. When a team has over-learned this move, plus counters, to keep the defense honest, it makes a tough assignment to defense the weave motion. Knowing the weave, practicing the slips, keeping the pass lanes contested with superior hustle by inside defenders, the defenders would have a good defense counter.

The defense should work hard to keep opponents frozen into weaves with nothing happening as far as penetration is concerned. The defenders of the two inside flashing posts should stay ballside and not allow a pass-in.

The defenders against the weave should maintain the spacing through the hand-off area to lead opponent by a shoulder width past the screen, which will eliminate a sudden turn to the basket by the offensive player. The defender of the hand-off man should be alert for a roll toward the basket by his hand-off opponent.

The defender against the hand-off player should be doubly alert to guard his opponent when he pulls away from hand-off to come back over on the next roll. The defender's opponent may go backdoor going away, or he may go backdoor coming back. Intensity in guarding this move is the answer. The same is true if the weave dribbler comes down to pick up the corner man. The corner player may elect a backdoor or a fake backdoor, then go back over the top of the ball.

The guard should be doubly alert as his man hesitates in coming over to the hand-off instead of going on. His opponent may reverse, thus catching the guard moving in the wrong direction.

A frequent non-ballside mistake is made by the defender, against the offense player, after the hand-off has been made and the passer moves away from the screen to time his coming back in over the next hand-off. The second defender's mistake is in staying inside of the offensive player, anticipating his coming back for the ball, only to have him reverse and break clear for a pass and the basket.

Watch out for the backdoor drives and the receiver of a hand-off reversing his motion and driving for the basket. Sometimes the dribbler slows down to hand off and with a change of pace continues on in for a drive lay-up. Defenders must concentrate on the movements that can come off the weave at the corners and at all hand-offs.

Once the defender's man moves away from hand-off, the defender should look for the pass inside, and from time to time move into the dribbler's lane position to push him out of the weave path. This will keep opponents from backing the defense right back to the free throw line. The defensing guard might try to two-time and jump-switch on the hand-off.

The defender should be alert for a bounce pass from the dribbler to the corner man and a cut for the basket in a give-and-go move. The defender of the corner man takes a position close enough inside and slightly ahead of the corner when coming out. He should put the pressure on a long pass and be ready to release and stop the backdoor.

The defender should have the same speed as the weaver and not overlead or underlead the motion.

He should drop off and two-time if the offensive man gets away. To become proficient in handling the screen and to keep position, the players should work! work! work! and talk! talk! talk! *and overlearn*. They should keep the hands in a position to pressure at all times and not go for the ball unless it's seventy-five percent exposed. Opponents want the guard to foul. The guard must work his close arm to mirror the ball and keep his shoulder ahead of his opponent.

When any offense dribbler breaks free off the weave, the inside defenders should ball position, stop the dribbler, and keep the strong inside pass lanes covered. The defenders on the weave should collapse quickly to pick up and pressure the weak-side pass lanes. They should arrive as the pass starts.

Some defensive men will close the space guarding the dribbler. This is the exact move the offense wants. It picks off defense's own teammate. Remember the *backs of the offense are TO the basket* so defense doesn't have to worry about shots.

Defense should execute its jump-switch and ball-pushing by surprise. The regular defense moves three or four times, then hits the opposition with the ball going away from the basket. Two-timing the corner hand-off is another spot for the surprise move. Great concentration, equal movement, hustle, and aggressive action will cut down on what the offense is trying to accomplish by weaving.

PRESSURING STATIONARY AND MOVING STACK PATTERNS WITH FLEXIBLE POSITIONING

The stack offense, with interchange of players in the stack, shows the defense the importance of teaching each player the specific tools that can be used to counter the pattern.

Again the ballside position is important, and spacing against it will allow a move up and down through the screens. There are double and triple stacks in general use to set up a good shot. This pattern alone cannot win a game but it makes it difficult to defense opponents who can score 6 or 10 points with the stack. If the double or triple stack is tied to a good movement of the offensive team, the defensive problem will be greater.

The most common stack is at the side of the key near the basket which gives the defense less time to slip screens and to cover the short shots. Diagrams will show some team defensive moves to aid in stopping the stack.

It is of the utmost importance that defenders against the standing screens keep in motion at all times. They must watch their man at all times but be sure to put a *good part of their vision on the ball movement*. To have eyes on man alone is fatal.

Set your defense to eliminate the inside shots and to keep good rebound checkout positions.

Defense must first cover all cutters ballside coming down into the key and low post area.

Flexible positioning is extremely important. *The defenders against the post screens must see the ball at all times.*

All defenders who drop to the key to stop all the inside penetration should be alert to move out on assignment quickly if the opponent moves or the ball starts toward the opponent. Every player should keep the ball in sight. And he should never take his eye completely away from the stack defense assignment. He should keep his feet in motion and not be lulled to sleep, or a sudden movement gives the opponent the ball position. Don't let the offensive man go over you to the ball position. Force him down.

Defense team should talk! talk! talk! And practice running through the defense moves until they are over-learned by all the squad members who are playing.

These defense experiences may give some ideas and thoughts about toughening your defensive procedures. *Don't get mechanical in countering the stack basic moves, or your players will be going down the key when their assignment is turning high up the key.*

Diagram 12-9. These plays (9, 10, and 11) illustrate a continuous weak side-strong side double stack attack. The stack is set by O5 moving to weak side and O2 moving down the key to the position at the top of the stack.

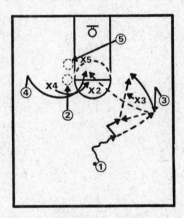

Diagram 12-9

This pattern can be continued with wings changing sides and the stack men O2 and O5 moving to the ball. O1, passing the ball to wing O3, receives a quick pass-in return, with O3 going backdoor to the basket. X3, the defender, should not get caught pulling up too tight and failing to execute a jump-back release as O3 starts his move to the basket. O4 starts to time his cut over the high post from the weak side as O1 starts his dribble toward the key if the pass lane is open. X4 should beat O4 over the double screen. If O4 goes to the baseline with X4 on top, X4 should flash down to the basket. O1 may pass to O4 or to O3. O3 may pass to late timing O4 who is coming over the screen, or pass back to O1 for a give-and-go.

Diagram 12-10. X3 must hold an inside ball position on O3 to the middle of the key, then drive up the lane to contest the pass to O3. Low screen X5 and high screen X2 should space above opponent and release sufficiently to let X3 up the key quickly. X5 and X2 should be alert for O5 and O2 changing positions or stepping away from the key for a pass.

O1 receiving the pass back from O3 will try to hit O4 coming over the double post screen. O2 follows O4's movement and posts in top of the key to get the pass from O1. O1 will drive over O2 to receive hand-off. X2 should move up with O2 pressuring the pass lane. X1 on the pass should execute a jump-back release that limits O1 the opportunity to go over the top of post O4. This eliminates the non-pressure screen shot, or a free drive to the baseline and the basket.

Diagram 12-11. This reverses the pattern flow with O3 going down through the key and up behind the double screen. O1 re-

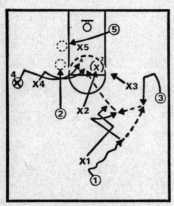

Diagram 12-10

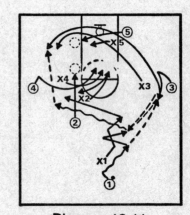

Diagram 12-11

verses with the dribble timed with O3's move and passes to O3 for a shot. X3 should beat O3 across the key in order to force O3 to keep moving. X1 should be in position and alert for X1 to go all the way with a dribble. O1 can stop and reverse dribble. X2 should be the key to flexible defense, ready to help in case O1 tries the inside move.

The flexible defense should understand the potential moves coming off of the three-man stack offense. Practice! Practice! Use variations that will keep the individual defenders honest.

Diagram 12-12. This illustrates the one basic move off of the strong side in the stack. O1 and O2 are the playmakers. O5 is at the low position with O4 taking the middle three-man stack position. O3 fakes the wing penetration play, then moves to the top of the stack.

O2 has flashed down through the key, coming out using the low screener O5. O2 drives for the open spot to receive a pass for the shot. Playmaker O1 driving toward the sideline may pass to O2, or reverse and drive over the top of the screener O3, or pass to break-out posts O4 or O5. X4 leads O4 to screen position, alert to go out ballside if O4 pulls out. X3 should be ballside of O3 as O3 goes to the stack. X5 should be alert ballside for a pullout of O5. X1 pressuring playmaker O1 should try to force O1 to the weak side where defenders have the greatest support.

Diagram 12-13. This illustrates the variation with stack low post moving out to receive the pass with O2 reversing back to the

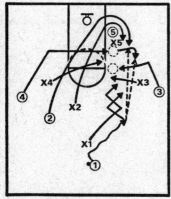

Diagram 12-12

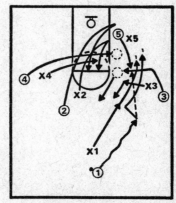

Diagram 12-13

basket. O3 will pull up out of the stack as a safety valve if the defenders stop the pass to the low post. O3 can hit O2 coming back under the basket. If X3 is high on O3 at the stack, the play is countered with a pass to O5 and with O1 flashing down on outside to receive the hand-off. X5 and X1 should have position with X1 going over the top.

Diagram 12-14. The only change is the pop-out of O4 from the stack to receive the ball. O4 can shoot in front of the screener O5, or double pass back to O1 who reverses and drives to the weakside. Or he can hit O2 coming up. X2 is the key. He should be ahead and have a ballside position as he comes back underneath across the key. O2 reversing back underneath the basket is taking advantage of the stack pressure and of the usual defensive error of getting beat crossing the key at low post. X1 should hold his position on O1 and not turn him free for a pass or an inside move.

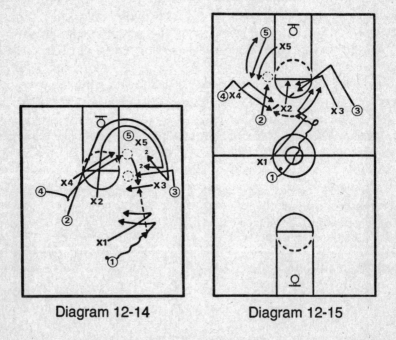

Diagram 12-14   Diagram 12-15

Diagram 12-15. This illustrates the fake to the weak side and a sudden reverse penetration to the strong side. Playmaker O1 starts his penetration just the same way. O3 acts out the same move, and

O4 starts his over-the-top of the double screen. O1 suddenly reverses as O4 fakes his way into the double screen. He then releases back toward the O1 playmaker for a pass. The move breaks both ways with O3 posting at top of the key weak side. O1 passes, reverses his drive to go outside the high post O3. As pass starts to O4, O5 comes up outside of the screener O2, giving O4 two ways to break play, passing either to post O3, or to O5. The pattern may add double cutters over either post O2 and O3, or over O3 or O5 with O1 cutting around post O5. Again X1 should really pressure the playmaker O1. X3 should attack the pass lane of O4 to O3 from the inside, but adjust quickly to stop the reverse drive by post O3.

X4 should be sure to have the top of the screen position and harass the pass lane. X2 plays loose and may put pressure on the pass lane to O3. X5 should tighten, ready to go out with O5, then protect the board. All defenders maintain inside ball positions, forcing the play to the outside. X1 and X2 are keys. X1 should have ballside on the cutter O1, and X2 should spoil the inside passes.

13

Flexible Man-to-Man Team Defenses, Conditioning, and Testing

To prepare for the coming league season you need to *choose a dominant league offensive pattern* which must be learned well by your squad. If you teach the proper individual defensive skills and the team defensive skills, you can control and counter this offensive pattern. It will be the same as putting money in the bank because you can draw on it for solving future defensive problems.

FLEXIBLE POSITIONING AND SPACE RELEASES IN DEFENSIVE PATTERN PREPARATION

Most teams run two or more offensive patterns closely related but different enough to change timing, change pass lanes, change shot areas, and change screen positions. This forces the defense to do double duty in the week's preparation for the game.

The defense should counter with two or more solid defenses which will cause the opposition to spend half its time preparing against a defense that might not be used. Such strategy should bring the teams into the game about even in game preparation.

The game test should show the best skilled in offensive and defensive tools the winner—that is if condition, will-to-win, experience, size, and speed are about equal. Best defense and best passing with fair shooting can put your team near the top.

All successful coaches work out unique variations of basic basketball fundamentals. All coaches throughout the country and the world have had access to the total knowledge of the game. You might think that all phases of the game would be the same, but the coaching approach has been as wide as the number of individual coaches who teach the skills to the players.

Putting the individual pieces together can be illustrated with diagrams of *team movement with ball motion around the perimeter with post defense fronting medium post.*

Diagrams 13-1, 13-2, 13-3. Low post motion, wing motion, and wing guard motions. These will help to explain the coordinated movement of individuals forming a tight-knit key defense and to illustrate the flex team defensive movement. These diagrams review the development given in Chapter 6 of flexible man-to-man team development because it is basic to the book's objectives.

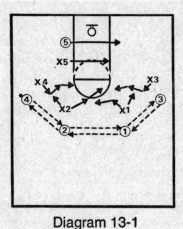

Diagram 13-1

Diagram 13-2

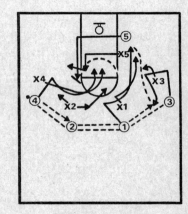

Diagram 13-3

To repeat: Defensive tempo can be mechanical just the same as the offense. But *your tempo goal is motion equal to or better than any the offense can produce.*

Condition your defense for a maximum team tempo that will stand up against the offenses'. High school games illustrate many times the fact that if the offense gets a lead but tires and slows down to the defensive team's mechanical pace, the game will remain even the rest of the way. *Challenge your defensive team's capacity to develop the most efficient tempo. Work all the time to improve individual and team defense skills for continuous tempo development.*

The ebb and flow of a game can hinge on the rise and fall of offensive and defensive tempos of both teams.

If you allow the tempo to groove, it will become mechanical without the necessary skill to counter a faster offense. The same efficient skills forced to move at a more rapid pace, *without practice*, will be unsuccessful at the new tempo level. Balances will change, spacing will change, and especially timing over screens. Movement in and away from the basket will force new position changes in order to counter the new tempo.

This may account for a defense being good against a team running shuffle in comparison to failure against another team running the same shuffle offense at a faster tempo.

DEFENSE CONDITIONING AND ITS RELATIONSHIP TO TOTAL GAME CONDITION BALANCE

For continuity in your season's planned practices, you should consider defensive conditioning build-up. The conditioning program should guarantee improvement to handle the game tempo and skill output throughout the *practice* season, all *done at game tempo increases.* Many games are won by the team that is in the best playing condition.

Many games are lost because of faulty weekly workouts. In college basketball there is a tendency to over-rest in game preparation, especially in the second half of the season. In high school any rest, or the placing of less emphasis on running condition tone, should be done during the midweek.

Condition your squad to work quickly and aggressively the night before the game. Experiment early in the season to find out how much work is needed to put players in good starting form, enough to carry them through the fourth quarter. This amount will change some as the season progresses. Be sure to aim for plus condition to handle teams with top four-quarter tempo.

Don't let the team loaf on the day after an early midweek game. The next day will be like blue Monday after Sunday's rest. You actually rebuild running condition into legs by exercising. It takes three times as long if you rest the players.

Continue reaffirming your position on training defense conditioning. After the skills of flexing, spacing, and positioning are attained, the tone and tempo should be kept at the highest capacity level *throughout* the season with challenging goals to be accomplished week after week.

Set aside the necessary minutes every day for the defense drills that best hold and develop your squad's maximum tone. One day's lay-off can make a difference in defensive alertness, quickness, and in continuous increase of toning and tempo.

Set your basic speed and endurance drills for the training season, then add variations during the season to offset monotony and to add challenges for steady improvement.

Remember your competitive quick drills across the key—high and low, fake-and-dribble, on the arc, fast out pressure away from the basket, fast drop from high to low post, speed pressure the length of the court, pickup fast mail at the ten-second line, and matching lateral and vertical speed drills. Add your endurance condition drills by stopwatch limits in lateral and advance retreat; follow all the floor lines over the full court working all the foot patterns; work against continuous three-man weave; and defense the dribbler on continuous two-to-four full court position play against the dribbler.

These efficient tools combined into well-knit team defense are the answer for controlling offenses.

The Decision on Defense-Offense Balance. The balance or emphasis between the offense and the defense is the most important decision to be made by a coach. The shooting and dribbling on offense generally is more advanced in most players because of their exposure to it in playground recreation and even on home courts.

Shooting is the early thrill part of the game. Dribbling too is fun. Trying to advance the ball as far as possible in order to get the ball in a shooting position is fun. These are essentials. But playground dribbling does not start good team play action. Rather it negates team assistance by not passing off to players who are open. All coaches have seen high school teams that can dribble well individually but who turn over the ball on attempted passes. Or dribble into trouble. Passing is the basis of most team efforts to advance the ball and to get open shots.

The dribble is important but the players should put it down only if a wide open lane confronts them, or use it to open closed pass lanes for their teammates. Every time a player retrieves the ball he must look up court for his teammates before going into a dribble.

Because *defense* has not been stressed early in a player's experience, coaches must sell the important role of defense and stay with it.

Defense is not only late in being learned but it takes more time to develop.

The thrill, fun, and satisfaction of playing defense must come from the competitive spirit and the challenge, for this is the part of the game that fights for the ball and pressures to control the offensive scoring penetration.

Let your offense get two points, but have the defense make your opponents pay and pay in work, time, and turnover opportunities before they get the two points back.

Coaches should examine the skills of each member of the squad for board defense, for inside and outside speed, for defense experience, and for combinations of players that would give the best defensive balance.

Early in your fall practice session try to keep a defensive chart on the development of each player. Sometimes defense progress is rapid at the start, then flattens out only to move ahead as details are mastered.

Every two or three weeks try to predict, or make an assessment, of your team's progress toward the development of a solid defense. *Don't sell individuals short at any time*. One player may be ahead in the second week, then another player will come on like a blockbuster.

ANALYZING, TESTING, AND CHARTING
INDIVIDUAL AND TEAM PROGRESS

Realizing that successful teaching must battle the time clock and the allotted number of days for pre-season practice, coaches should organize their practices carefully. They must place time limits on the learning of various skills.

Possibly a chart showing the amount of time to be allotted to offensive patterns, rebounding, shooting, out-of-bounds, held balls, passing, dribbling, and defenses, will help efficient distribution according to your squad's strengths and weaknesses.

Review the various time-saving skill information sheets about your new squad and its individual player's experiences. A second chart rating each individual on the squad according to his experience and performance during the past season will be helpful in weighing skill abilities and in formulating the drills for practice.

In planning to use the man-to-man flexible style of defense, it is important that you set up a list of fundamentals and details that need to be executed successfully against the post and screen patterns of your opposition.

Rate the skills according to the importance in developing the team defense to counter your oppositions' patterns successfully. Test each individual player's ability to successfully execute each fundamental skill during scrimmage pressure.

Develop a chart that will show each player where his strengths or weaknesses are in the execution of the fundamental skills. Use a rating of one to ten for comparative skill execution.

Diagram 13-4. This pictorial illustration of skill success and rate of learning can be developed for the fundamental offensive skills as well as the defensive part of the game.

This charting and rating gives the player a pictorial position of his skills and his rate of advancement in developing the defensive fundamentals necessary in the execution of good team defense.

By observing scrimmages and focusing on individual weaknesses or mistakes, you will develop your ability to mentally review total defensive games.

If you do not use movies, use your eye to photograph and recall, then write out short individual reports.

ONE ON ONE DEFENSE
EXPANDED PRESSURE DEFENSE
RUNNING LANE DEFENSE
OVER THE TOP DEFENSE
SLIP THE SCREEN DEFENSE
REBOUNDING
BALL SIDE DEFENSE
SINK SIDE DEFENSE
CENTER OR POST DEFENSE
WING DEFENSE
PERIMETER DEFENSE
FULL COURT PRESSURE
GUIDING
SPACING
RELEASING
HAND ACTION
POSITIONING
COURT MOTION
ANGLE SHUFFLE
VERTICAL SHUFFLE
LATERAL SHUFFLE
PIVOTS
ONE COUNT STOPS
STANCE STARTS

JOHN FORD

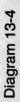

Diagram 13-4

Players like to have concrete, individual, positive criticisms to work on at teaching stations or in their spare time.

Every coach should take four to six weeks of summer planning each year to program the new squad needs and the ways to meet these needs in an organized time schedule for successful teaching and *over-learning* of the fundamentals of team defenses.

Reading or going to a clinic to pick up even one defensive aid to fit into your own successful scheme of defensive play, you will find worth the effort if it advances your team's defensive toughness.

Going from the information board, oral explanation, to the drill, to the scrimmage and then to the game condition you will be taking the steps of greatest importance for the squad's success to make these transitions in the allotted time given to develop the tough team defense.

The coach's job is to organize and to teach the skills to insure the squad's progress in an orderly and *on time* manner as directed by his master, and weekly, schedules without infringing upon other learning phases of the game.

Such effort is the only way to keep on an even keel with the total game instruction and have a balanced readiness for the first practice game trial run.

Never give up on selling and teaching the basic tools of defensive play, even though defense inexperience dictates choosing combination defenses to hide a temporary weakness.

Give every player a daily chance to develop more tools to enhance his contribution to the total team defensive play. Master one solid defensive pattern that your starting five and the next three or four substitutes can successfully execute. If your subs can come in and maintain the solid defense, you need not worry too much about their ability to score. But if your opponents put a hole in your defensive dike, you'd better have a hot shot coming in who will stop the tide or at least keep up with the opposition.

The defensive portrait of each individual defender can be an important positive pressure that helps him understand his defensive contribution in terms of points. This puts the defensive part of the game on a par with the offense.

Once you establish your flexible defensive program, the next year will be easier. To start a tradition is a great motivational aid for both the coach and the players.

POSITIVE PLUS AND NEGATIVE MINUS POINTS
SCORING PORTRAIT

Stealing ball	+1	Fouling	−1
Forcing turnovers	+1	Not pressuring shot	−1
Rebounding ball	+1	Forcing teammate to switch	−½
Forcing a foul	+1	Losing man on baseline	−1
Stopping the teammate's assignment	+1	Not pressuring opponent's ball movement	−1
Hand action tagging a pass	+½	Not talking	−½
Forcing ball to weakest position	+½	Not pressuring opponent out 16′	−½

The most difficult part of defense is to learn the details, but they are the keys to a tough defense. Individual development will depend on a player's interest span and his ability to concentrate. Hard work and the selling of the importance of self-discipline to the individual players are great aids to progress. Short five-minute talks on one important skill at a time will greatly help the floor learning speed.

Pride in successful endeavor and confidence are both essential.

An aggressive approach and the relishing of a challenge are part of a flexible defense success. This flexible man-to-man defense should give you some answers to the development of the soundest part of basketball.

Index